What are People Saying About This Book?

This is *the* book! If you are the person in your organization who needs to get the job done, not just discuss the theory, then this is the book. The authors tell how a Lean Enterprise looks, how to get there and the pitfalls to look for along the way. They tell you where you will find the most benefit, and where you will find the money when you become a Lean company. **It is readable, understandable and it is excellent. The pages in my copy are marked up in yellow, underlined and dog-eared.** If you were afraid to try Lean before you read the book, you will put this down at the end thinking, "I must do this." And, having read the book, you will say, "And now I know how."

- Posted by "Marilyn from PPI" on Amazon.com

I have just finished this book and it is excellent! This is **not just another book on Lean.** This is an indictment of executives, managers and concrete heads in organizations that aspire to mediocrity. These authors have obviously been in the trenches and understand what most of us go through as we try to implement this process. There is **great advice and hard-hitting commentary** on why companies are failing to get the full benefits of Lean. Check out the *Lean Math* Chapter where Offshore Outsourcing is compared to a Lean alternative. Executives and managers have a huge responsibility and they are not (from what I experience) living up to it. The authors explain why engagement is critical as well as commitment. **Management should read this book** and then ask themselves a lot of tough questions. Also, the whole discussion on education and institutionalization is right on the money. [...] You are going Lean or you are not going anywhere, and this book shows why you need to do it before you are forced into it by your customers or your competition. I hope these guys write another book. **This is a breath of fresh Lean air.**

-Peter Square, Wexford, PA

If you want to avoid the mistakes that most companies make when implementing Lean then this book is a must. I have had the good fortune to attend one of the extensive seminars by these authors and they really know their stuff. They have great stories to tell and their experiences are recounted in this book. As you read through the Elusive Lean Enterprise you can understand why many companies don't implement Lean successfully. I have read most of the Lean books out there and this is one of the best.

- Jack Beale, a Lean practitioner

The Elusive Lean Enterprise

Keith E. Gilpatrick & Brian Furlong

Second Edition

Multi-Media
Publications Inc.
Oshawa, Ontario

The Elusive Lean Enterprise

By Keith E. Gilpatrick and Brian Furlong

Managing Editor:	Kevin Aguanno
Copy Editor:	Josette Coppola
Typesetting:	Tak Keung (Charles) Sin
Cover Design:	Troy O'Brien

Published by:
Multi-Media Publications Inc.
Box 58043, Rosslynn RPO, Oshawa, Ontario, Canada, L1J 8L6

http://www.mmpubs.com/

ISBN-10/13 (Paperback):   1-897326-64-5 / 9781897326640
ISBN-10/13 (Hardcover):   1-897326-65-3 / 9781897326657
ISBN-10/13 (Adobe PDF eBook):   1-897326-66-1 / 9781897326664
ISBN-10/13 (Mobipocket PRC eBook): 1-897326-67-X / 9781897326671

Published in Canada. Printed simultaneously in U.S.A. and England.

CIP Data available from the publisher.

Contents

The Need for Change 115

Institutionalizing Lean 151

Lean in a Non-Manufacturing Enterprise 251

Lean for Healthcare 263

Dedication

This book, as well as past and future ventures, is dedicated to Brian's wife Jill for her unwavering support and assistance.

Acknowledgements

We would like to acknowledge the following individuals for their questions, advice, assistance and time while editing *The Elusive Lean Enterprise.*

We are very grateful for the interest they have shown and the support that they continue to give.

- Karen E. Airulla – President, K.E.E. Strategies

- Paul J. Paparone – Vice president (ret.) Human Resources, Emerson

- W. Kip Speyer – Former CEO, Galileo Corp. and ICAD

- Joan Gilpatrick, CPA – Director of Finance, Getronics

Foreword to the Second Edition by Dolf Kahle

Lean is a culture, not a flavor of the month. Lean is a simplistic approach to help any organization improve its performance. The principles of Lean have existed for decades in the manufacturing environment. Just witness Henry Ford's moving assembly line to eliminate numerous wastes as defined by the '8 Wastes of Lean.'

So why did it take so long for us to grab hold of it? Maybe it was because no one had systematically written down its principles until the publishing of the *The Toyota Way*. The Japanese didn't invent a new improved methodology; they just looked for the obvious and documented their procedures.

I was fortunate to have a great mentor in my father, Hermann Kahle. In the early 80s, he acquired a very small printing company (one printing press). My stroke of luck was when he asked me to join him to build our small company that would eventually become one of the top 10 companies in the U.S. in our specialty: manufacturing and supplying durable product identification to the American OEM market (decals, nameplates, labels, and overlays). We had no quality manual, no documented procedures, and no one trained to produce a more sophisticated product than the simple truck decals we were selling (we actually only produced 25% of what we sold). So Hermann began our journey to become a Lean Enterprise by writing a simple quality assurance manual that began with First Article Inspection (quality at the source). Over the next 15 years, he taught me Preventive Maintenance, Quick Change Over Drills, Standardized Procedures, Point of Source Inventory (Kanban), the team approach to solving problems (Kaizen), factory layout (Spaghetti Charts)… and this was long before *The Toyota Way* was published.

Fast forward to 2006. My company was growing and successful. And we experienced all the same global pressures as any industry: customers demanding lower prices, reduced lead times, rising raw material prices, rising employee benefits, and our customer's expectation was "perfection." We needed to kick-start our own "Better, Faster, and Cheaper" program. How could I excite our staff to find new solutions to improving our bottom line?

That is where Brian and Keith stepped into our future. I was looking for a simple approach to Lean that would educate and train all our employees (and spark the management staff). Their book, *The Elusive Lean Enterprise,* and their *Lean Mastery* software became our Lean Enterprise University. We trained our initial 20 champions and 11 managers on their Lean principles. We kick started our program with a dynamic Lean seminar directed by Brian. He supplied tools to document our Lean progress.

But before I hired Lean Enterprise Inc., I had to share this book with Hermann. Once he finished reading it, we had a great conversation retracing our past 25 years together growing our business. The principles weren't new to us. But they recalled our many strategies that led to many successes: our path to becoming a Lean Enterprise before we knew what Lean really was. And Hermann found the book to be well grounded in effective principles to improve any organization's bottom line.

As I said before, I was fortunate to have my own Lean guru long before this book was published. Now you can have your Lean gurus in Brian Furlong and Keith Gilpatrick and their *Lean Mastery* program. Read it, absorb it, and then teach it to all you encounter that need to eliminate waste, improve their productivity and flourish in this highly-competitive global market.

Dolf Kahle
Chief Executive Officer
Visual Marking Systems
www.vms.com

Foreword by Keith Gilpatrick

Some years ago, Brian and I were up to our necks in Lean Enterprise transformations at companies spread all over the globe. At that time, we were experiencing a multitude of physical and mental maladies, caused by poorly-executed Lean implementation plans and the insane, although common, strategy of trying to generate cash, and profits, from manufacturing operations that could not meet the lofty expectations from "stretch goals" placed on them by corporate management. Along with many others, I was fooled into thinking that the merits of Lean combined with a corporate mandate, and that the vitality of a few would be adequate to energize the corporation and power the engine of change. All was not lost, however. There were many success stories as we journeyed through these Lean transformations. There were plants that became Lean and, in the spirit of Kaizen,[1] were continuing to improve. There were processes in plants that were significantly improved, and provided products with "five nines" quality, at a greatly reduced total cost, while meeting required delivery dates. There were people in corporate and plant organizations who grasped the Lean concepts and contributed greatly to the successes. However, the corporation itself failed to create a Lean organization.

This book is not about the failure of any particular company to become Lean. Since our departure from our prior company, Brian and I have been Lean Enterprise consultants and continue to experience the same limiting issues. While we present Lean concepts, we did not want to write a book solely for that purpose. *The Elusive Lean Enterprise* is intended to provoke Lean thinking, and provide guidelines for a successful Lean Enterprise implementation.

In this foreword, I urge you to look backward. The one thing every executive should do before attempting a Lean transformation is to look *backward* through the history of the operation and identify *results* and *behaviors* that got them where they are today. Some questions to ask during this trip into history are

- Have we been realistic in our expectations (on both sales and net profit forecasts)?

- Were our processes capable of delivering the desired results?

- Have we been good planners?

- Did we have the right people to execute our plans?

---

[1] Kaizen means continuous incremental improvement. Kaizen is also the name given to the project or project team established to review a process and improve that process using Lean concepts. Kaizen is the engine that powers the Lean transformation.

- Did we have the corporate infrastructure to execute our plans?

- Were we oversized or undersized with regard to equipment?

- Did we understand Value as perceived by our customers?

- Have we been a good supplier to our customer base?

- Were we *leaders* or *followers* in our industry?

- Do we understand what quality costs in our company?

- What were we the best at?

- What were we the worst at?

- How quickly did we react to changes in the marketplace?

- Was there a metric that drove results (productivity, quality, cost)?

- Did we provide our people with everything they needed to produce results (education, leadership, money, equipment, goals, guidelines, etc.)?

- Did we work with (or cope with) our suppliers?

- What drove our research and design efforts?

- Where did we spend our profits and what was the payback?

- Are our successors present in the company?

- Who helped the most?

- Who let us down?

- Did we lead or manage our results?

- How would a good idea reach my desk?

- Which did we do best: talk or listen?

- Have we outsourced core competencies? If so, what has the impact been?

- Have we lost customers? If so, why?

I could go on and on with these questions. The point that needs to be made is that these questions should always be on the mind of an executive who is interested in growth and profitability. As markets change and demand for products evolve, management must respond.

While there are probably an equal number of questions you should ask yourself when planning a Lean transformation I will leave those questions for you to develop as you read *The Elusive Lean Enterprise.*

Foreword by Brian Furlong

When I first met Keith, I had just been assigned the responsibility for the Lean implementation at my 13-plant division, in addition to all of my other duties as V.P. of Operations. I was reluctant to participate in what, I then believed, was yet another 'program of the month.' However, I quickly went from being an unwilling student to an enthusiastic promoter once I understood the sheer power and potential of a Lean enterprise.

If Lean Enterprise concepts were presented to a college student with no manufacturing experience, that student would likely wonder about all the fuss. The Lean process is so logical that the student would likely think that it is in general use. Reality is very different. For those of us who have been involved with manufacturing for some time, there is much work to be done to eliminate the waste that has crept into our processes over many years.

Despite the obvious benefits, true Lean Enterprises are few in number. That is why we have titled this book *The Elusive Lean Enterprise*. As we set about the process of becoming Lean in a number of companies in many different countries, it became clear that there were key factors that were preventing a successful Lean implementation. We address these factors in this book and present a challenge to management to take a different look at the process and the speed of the Lean transformation. Management commitment is critical to the success of almost any program, and Lean is no different. However, for a successful Lean implementation, management engagement is also required. It is not enough to provide the moral support, or even the financial resources. Management must be involved in the process every day so that the priorities stay in focus, the effort is properly aligned, the financial resources are wisely applied, and the payback is real.

Most businesses have spent decades institutionalizing the way things are done today. Why then would you think that we do not need to institutionalize Lean? The Lean transformation requires a culture change, and yet many companies spend little effort in attempting to change the culture. Changing the culture to Lean is a long-term endeavor. Yet, in many companies, it is assumed that Lean will stand on its own merits and that people will automatically jump aboard. This simply does not happen. We will address both the need for change and the process of change in this book.

Another major issue is what we call the 'need-to-know syndrome.' For some inexplicable reason companies treat their employees like they worked for the CIA. They provide only limited education on Lean and then strictly on a need-to-know basis. If you want a successful Lean transformation, you must have everyone in your company educated on *all* aspects of Lean. Employees have much more to contribute than just the knowledge of their own work area. If you fail to harness, and motivate, this critical resource, you will surely have very limited success.

This is not just another book on the technical aspects of Lean, even though we do review briefly the elements, rules and tools. This book is intended to reflect on the mistakes that companies make in failing to address the critical implementation issues. Those who have had Lean success will tell you that Lean is a journey, not a destination. In every journey, there is an opportunity to take a wrong turn or to get off-track. This book will help to keep you on course so that the journey itself becomes the destination.

As a passionate advocate of Lean, it is frustrating to see the low rate of Lean success. The Lean process itself is not the problem. Those of us who have had success have proven that the potential benefits are astonishing. The problem is that many companies want the result without the effort. This is like saying that you want to win the lottery but you don't want to buy a ticket. One thing is certain: if you are not *in*, you cannot *win*. With Lean, if you do not want to put in the investment, you will not get the results.

Finally, Keith and I have devoted the remainder of our careers to the practice and promotion of Lean. Having spent many years doing things the *'wrong way,'* we understand the full potential for companies who believe that there is little remaining opportunity to improve profitability, competitiveness or growth. You can avail of the Lean opportunity by avoiding the pitfalls, and by learning from the mistakes of others. This book is worthwhile if we help just one business to benefit from Lean.

About This Book

Management works in the system.
Leadership works on the system.
Dr. Steven Covey

A merica did not evolve as a leader in world commerce as it did in the 20th century by riding the backs of intellectuals. While we would be the first to acknowledge the intellectual contributions, this book is more about the adaptability of visionary leaders and the ingenuity and tenacity of the workers who participated in the building of America's industries. America began with a group of people who welcomed the opportunity to work hard and change their lot in life. The requirements for survival in the early settlements were ingenuity and a strong back. Commerce was essential for providing the materials and services necessary for survival. The bartering system was strong back then. If you needed a shovel you would work hard to create a means to acquire that shovel. Towns grew from this system of exchange. Towns were simply teams of individuals with varying skills. No single individual, or primary skill, was responsible for the success of the enterprise. Visionary, courageous and unselfish leaders emerged; thinking primarily about what was good for the masses.

Change was the primary motivator for those who came to America. Immigrants thought that there was an opportunity for a better life, even though the risks, in those days, were significant. This book is about change. The same teamwork that was so effective in building America is viewed by the authors of this book as the key to our country's survival in the global market. We need business leaders with vision, and we need to dig deep into the enterprise to avail of the intelligence and ingenuity of the employees.

The systems and processes used to build and maintain our industries have become overly complicated and costly, making it difficult to meet the price needs of today's global marketplace. This situation exists even during times when productivity is high. Consequently, it has become increasingly more difficult to sustain the level of profits that keep investors on board.

Productivity is a metric tossed around by many as a key factor when evaluating the status and efficiency of U.S. industries. The primary problem with productivity as a measure is that the level of inventory in those industries being measured is usually proportionate to the increase or decrease in productivity. Being efficient and building inventory that does not seem to sell should be a concern for those wanting to compare U.S. industry performance with other countries based on productivity. High inventory levels in the U.S. is usually followed by layoff or downsizing announcements by those companies that are not moving their large on-hand finished goods inventories.

There is panic! In some companies, management is reacting to the tight margins by moving operations to low cost countries around the globe, or finding suppliers in those countries in an attempt to reduce their cost of goods sold. Downsizing is also a common strategy for those executives who are caught up in the margin improvement dilemma. The principal antagonist is considered by many to be the cost of labor.

We would not attempt to argue that labor costs are high in America. What we do dispute is that labor is the only cost one should consider. We will discuss the costs of elaborate, yet ineffective, processes that have crept into our business systems. We will discuss the talent of American management. Are we to believe that the only solution to the high cost of doing business in America is to leave? American management is compensated as high, if not higher, as any other in the world. Shouldn't we expect better performance from this stable of high cost executives?

What we won't discuss, yet contributes to the high cost of doing business in America is the cost of employee benefits and costs associated with taxes and litigation. These costs are growing rapidly and will require intervention by our State and Federal governments to lessen the burden.

Leading vs. Managing

We have heard it said a million times that successful people have, and need, large egos. We would agree with this statement in any situation where the goal is individual success. However, when the goal is the success of a group of individuals, or an enterprise, a strong ego alone will not ensure success. The confidence in oneself that is inherent with strong egos needs to be supplemented with selflessness, trust, responsibility, and vision. Leaders have all of these traits. We believe strongly that there is a significant difference between leaders and managers. The method used to create the following list was not scientific. It was developed from years of experience working with executives and managers in several different companies.

Characteristics

Leaders	Managers
Vision	Tunnel Vision
Participate	Dictate
React (tactical)	Act (theatrical)
Selfless	Egotistical
Group success	Individual success
Adapt	Retreat
Progress	Vegetate
Take responsibility	Place responsibility
Let go	Hold on
Talk	Scream
Walk the talk	Talk the talk

Believe	Doubt
Trust	Control
Laugh	Leer
Guide	Push
Change	Maintain
Influence (Others)	Sway on demand
Stay	Leave
Seek	Hide
Realize	Fantasize
Do	Meet
Plan	Plot
At the front	At the rear
Head up	Head down
Feed	Eat
Deploy	Hold fast
Create	Destroy
Motivate	De-motivate
Share	Hoard

Lean requires leadership, not management. You have to believe your goal is to change the culture of your enterprise, and to do this, you must take the lead and participate in the change process. People expect and want to be lead, not to be managed.

In military terms, a soldier will take a bullet for a leader and save a bullet for a manager. This is human behavior in the extreme but it should make the point clear. No one enjoys the risks or wants to suffer the consequences of being around a 'manager.'

If you are an executive currently contemplating a Lean transformation, look for those individuals who will help you lead the implementation and avoid those who will simply want the implementation managed. This book is about getting back to the basics. Lean focuses primarily on the processes that are used to conduct business. It is a totally integrated business process that is based on value, as defined by the downstream customer, and it seeks to eliminate any activity that does not add value. As the title suggests, Lean is elusive. We believe there are five primary reasons for this.

1. Management lacks a concise knowledge of the program, and does not consider Lean as a solution because they have not yet recognized, nor admitted, that it's their processes that are out of control.

2. When Lean is selected as an improvement program it is administered as exactly that – a program – and not a total change in the company culture. Senior executives do not give Lean the attention that is needed to have a successful implementation and a sustained continuous process improvement culture. The responsibility for (and active participation in) the Lean transformation is placed at too low a level in the organization. As a result, traditional management and operational philosophies slow (if not impede) a timely and effective implementation.

3. Lean is for everyone in the enterprise. However, educating to the lowest level in the organization, and implementing Lean through Kaizen events comprised of cross-functional, and low-level

employees, is difficult for some executives to allow. Certain types of executives view Lean as a threat to both their organization and authority. Additionally, there is the trait of 'wanting to influence the outcome' demonstrated by some that will cause problems in a Lean implementation.

4. The way change itself is managed.

5. Lean Enterprise evolved from the Toyota Production System and was considered by many to apply only to automotive companies and their suppliers, or other very large companies.

In our *Lean Mastery* course, we talk about managers who simply need to influence the outcome of everything that happens in business. The analogy that we use to explain this influencing trait is that there are two types of people in the world: those who push the "Elevator Door Close Button" and those who don't. We are not human behavior experts but we believe there is some logic in our hypothesis. Those who push the button, view the elevator as their personal vehicle, and fail to consider anyone else who may need to use it; nor do they have the patience to wait a few seconds for the programmed timing system to work. In the Lean world, these button pushers are often difficult people with whom to work. Such people find it difficult to work within systems that are programmed for the benefit of most, and will go to great lengths to maintain their personal influence over the outcome of any improvement program.

The challenge to executives is to recognize when their processes no longer provide products and services that can compete effectively in the global marketplace. Albert Einstein is credited with saying "To repeat the same thing over and over and expect that the results will change is insanity". Executives need to challenge their operating management to redefine value based on the needs of their customers and examine the processes currently in use to determine if those processes are capable of providing value and returning an acceptable profit. Lean is for executives who want to create and fix; it is not for those executives who simply want to manage.

It's the process, not the people

Our use of the words "manager, management, and manages" in this text indicates a title, function, or activity; not that we aspire to the definition that could be created using our characteristics list.

1

The Lean Enterprise

> Some say the glass is half full;
> others say the glass in half empty.
> Lean thinkers challenge the size of the glass.
> - *Keith Gilpatrick*

L ean is a process improvement strategy comprised of Elements, Rules and Tools. Lean focuses primarily on the elimination of waste from all business processes. A smaller yet no less important portion of Lean involves specific concepts that are intended to provide excellent quality products, delivered on time, at the lowest total cost, and only on the specific demand of the customer.

Perhaps the greatest injustice to Lean is that, early in its introductory phase, Lean was described as a variant of the Toyota Production System (TPS). This was done out of necessity by the authors of the book *Lean Thinking*.[1] Lean Enterprise concepts presented in *Lean Thinking* were developed by analyzing the way Toyota manufactured automobiles. While the authors continuously point out that the Toyota manufacturing concepts were applicable to any manufacturing or administrative process, we believe that associating Lean concepts with Toyota automatically limited its application in the minds of a great number of people. Lean was considered as a system of improvement for those companies involved in the direct manufacture of automobiles, or their direct suppliers. Additionally, the association with Toyota had many thinking that Lean was a program for large companies only. The early promoters of Lean concepts also placed too much emphasis on the Flow and Pull Elements of Lean resulting in the perception that Lean was a production improvement system.

If you attempt to promote Lean as a production system the response you will likely get is "Lean probably works well in the automotive industry, but it could not possibly work with our company because we do not manufacture automobiles, and our production process, and customer demands are very different." If Lean is promoted as a process improvement system that focuses on the elimination of waste from all processes, the response might be "how do you think you may be able to help us?"

---

[2] Womack, James P. and Daniel T. Jones. *Lean Thinking*. 1st Free Press ed., revised and updated. New York: Free Press, 2003.

Eight Types of Waste

Lean primarily focuses on the elimination of waste from all business processes. Each of the individual types of waste can be found in both manufacturing and administrative operations. The activities that are considered wasteful have crept into our business processes for any number of reasons. Key among those is the control mentality that requires review and approval of almost everything that is done in the organization. Additionally, there is the paranoia present that results in huge inventories because productivity is a metric used to measure manufacturing, and no one wants to be caught short of raw materials or finished goods inventory. Machinery and plant layouts also contribute to waste. Machines that are capable of producing faster than needed are often purchased because no one is conscious of, or concerned about, the speed of the entire process. These machines may also require changeover times of several hours to produce different parts. Consequently, large batches of material are often produced to justify the time and cost associated with the changeovers. Plant layouts often evolve around the size and noise level of the equipment. This frequently results in great distances between a machine and the next downstream process.

As you review the types of waste listed below, think of examples that apply to both manufacturing and administrative processes.

1. Mistakes which require rectification (rework; or worse, scrap).

2. Production of inventory that no one wants.

3. Processing steps that are not needed.

4. Unnecessary transport of material and sub-assemblies.

5. Unnecessary movement by employees active in the production process.

6. Groups of people in downstream processes waiting for the completion of upstream work.

7. Producing goods or services that do not meet the specific needs of customers.

8. Failure to fully utilize the time and talents of people.

The eight types of waste are fundamental concepts to keep in mind when implementing the elements and rules of Lean. Every Kaizen event that you conduct during your Lean transformation should include a checklist to indicate that all of the elements of waste have been considered as you review the current process, and as you create a new Lean process.

Mistakes that Require Rectification (Rework; or worse, Scrap)

Rework and scrap are most likely caused by either the lack of standard work instructions, or the discipline within production lines to follow formal work instructions, if they are available. Additionally, in cases where the process includes a final inspection by the quality department, an attitude can develop that people need not worry about the quality of their work because any mistakes made will be caught in final inspection.

It is also possible that the company itself has accepted that a certain level of scrap and rework is inevitable. This is an admission that the materials, or the processes used, are not the best, or that the company has not been able to correct supplier quality, or the process itself. We have worked for companies that are on perpetual quality control journeys. Rather than determine the root cause of process or material-related problems, they spent millions of dollars each year maintaining quality departments accommodating either poor suppliers or poor processes.

In the book *The Machine that Changed the World* (by James P. Womack, Daniel T. Jones, and Daniel Roos, published in 1991 by Harper Perennial), indications were that the space provided for rework at automotive manufacturing companies other than Toyota could be as much or equal to the total space used to manufacture by Toyota. The companies with large rework areas had accepted that mistakes in the production line were inevitable and chose to fix them at the end of the process. Toyota, on the other hand, would not let a mistake move down the line. They required that the production process be interrupted for the purpose of root cause analysis and a timely fix before production could continue.

No level of scrap or rework should be acceptable. The root cause should be determined, and a permanent fix should be implemented. Employees should view scrap and rework as evil. When this mentality is implanted into the company culture, you will experience huge financial benefits, and it is likely that your customer satisfaction statistics will also improve. Many companies have the misfortune of having their customers act as the final quality check. This is a costly gamble for both the company and the customer.

Production of Inventory that no one Wants

There are many reasons why companies produce inventory that is not shipped immediately to end customers. A small sample of these is shown below.

- Machine utilization is used as a performance metric.

- Direct labor hours produced (productivity) is used as a performance metric.

- Sales forecasts, used to feed Material Requirements Planning systems (MRP), are not reliable.

- Research and Development departments operate in a vacuum, and develop products that are not well received by customers.

- Marketing or sales people mistake a "single customer preference" for a broad market demand.

- Spikes in (or seasonal) demand.

- Acceptance of a particular inventory turn statistic as an industry standard.

Lean thinkers believe that inventory is evil. Everything that can be done must be done to eliminate the production of inventory that has no immediate demand. This requires a culture change within the supplier, company, and customer organizations that focuses on actual customer demand as opposed to productivity metrics. A careful and well-planned implementation of a Pull system will have a dramatic effect on inventory. Producing finished goods should be based on actual customer orders, and work-in-process inventory should be dictated by the Pull of parts and assemblies from the downstream processes. This, in turn, should signal the need for raw materials or purchased sub-assemblies from outside suppliers.

A goal that we frequently recommend to our clients is to plan the elimination of the current warehouse facility. If you need inventory, have it stored directly at the location where it will be used (Point of Use Inventory Storage). Inventory reduction should be a Policy Deployment Metric for any company attempting a Lean transformation. The inventory reduction aspect of Lean is one of the more difficult ones. A good experiment to conduct early in your planning phase is to get managers from every discipline in your company together and suggest that your goal is to reduce the inventory by half each year for the next three years. The result of this session will provide you with a great list of action items that you will need to incorporate into your implementation plans.

Processing Steps that are not Needed

Unnecessary processing steps can be a difficult element of waste to recognize. For the most part, you are accustomed to the way you process products or services. It can sometimes take a stranger to the process to question why things are done as they are today. A basic rule to follow relates to the value aspect of Lean Enterprise; if there is no value to the process step, then you should not perform that activity.

A fair amount of the administrative process activity is of no value to your end customer, and they are certainly not paying you to perform that effort. Over the years, financial controls, coupled with a lack of trust in employees to do the job right, have resulted in review and approval processes that add no value and have brought operations to a glacial pace. Consider that, with a little effort, the intended quality or control can probably be built into the process with little need for human review and approval.

Multiple inspections of parts and assemblies are a good example of process steps that are wasteful. The focus should be on working with outside suppliers, or in-house production departments to reach a high level of quality. Accepting that you will have poor quality from either your outside suppliers or in-house production departments may result in a quality cost structure that is difficult to eliminate.

Moving product around a plant is wasteful if the distance between sequential processes is not needed. Limiting the distance that material and people travel will be discussed later in the Rules section. For now, keep in mind that any movement of material or people that is not necessary will add time and costs to the process, and should be considered waste. Plant layouts are frequent targets of Lean improvement programs.

Unnecessary Transport of Material and Sub-assemblies

As we just mentioned, any movement of material and sub-assemblies in a process should be challenged. As you will see when you read about Flow, all process steps should be moved as close to each other as possible.

The concept of Flow is to establish a 'one-piece-flow' process by allowing a hand-off of individual parts and assemblies to the next downstream process. This is different to processing large batches before parts or assemblies are moved to the next downstream process. Lean Enterprise requires that items Flow through the plant at the demand of the downstream customer. This concept is known as the Pull system. Utilizing Flow and Pull will have a dramatic effect on material handling in a plant that is a typical mass manufacturing or batch-and-queue operation. A good example of this type of waste is an operation where raw material is stored in a warehouse, picked for delivery to a sub-assembly department, then who, after processing the transformed material is returned to the warehouse for a pick request that comes from a downstream process. In this situation, production departments are scheduled independently of actual customer demand in order to keep equipment and people productive. A significant amount of material handling and warehouse management resource is needed when you operate this way. Scheduling in this environment can also be a nightmare.

It is not uncommon to see that material moves through the entire process in different container sizes requiring multiple material transfers within the process to facilitate the next process step. The initial process may be performed on a pallet of material that is moved from the raw material storage area. Multiple pallets may then be required to store the resulting sub-assembly which may be placed in different containers for delivery to the next process, when requisitioned. Manufacturing in a non-Pull environment is typically burdened with significant material handling waste.

If you have spent any time in a warehouse, you will have noticed that material is constantly being moved due to a material locator system that expands and contracts based on the volume of material that is on hand. At times, it seems as though this activity is merely keeping warehouse employees busy.

Another example of wasteful material movement is the periodic inventory. Materials may have to be moved to weigh stations or counting stations to have the contents of boxes or containers verified. Lean Enterprise requires that material be stored at the location that will use the material (Point-of-Use Inventory Storage). When this method is used, a Kanban is established that has identical amounts contained in each batch. Conducting an inventory of this material can be done easily by multiplying the number of Kanbans by the standard Kanban quantity.

Unnecessary Movement by Employees Active in the Production Process

This type of waste focuses on the hand and foot movement made by workers who perform the process steps required. Wasteful movement is caused by unnecessary distances between the source of material, and the machines or workbenches in the production area. Additionally, turning and bending to work or to locate parts or assemblies is also wasteful. When you are organizing a production line or workbench for ease of use, you should make every attempt to limit movement. This type of waste is also very prevalent in the office. Employees often have to travel large distances to the next process step, or to utilize a common piece of equipment.

Visit any manufacturing facility and you will see wasteful movement by employees. There are many reasons for this and some are outlined below.

- Workbenches are oversized.

- Machines in a multiple machine process are not as close as they could be.

- Tools needed for the process are not always where they should be, and the tool storage set-up is not organized properly.

- Parts and assemblies used in the process are not stored for easy access.

- Processes that have material delivered on pallets, or large containers, require workers to vary their movement as the pallets or containers are emptied.

- Processed parts or assemblies placed into containers or onto pallets for movement to the next process also provide for varied movement.

When you visit a manufacturing facility and notice that there are a lot of people walking around, this is a good indication that people, machines, materials, and tools are not located in an efficient manner.

Accepting current container sizes, workbench sizes, and tool storage methods can limit your creativity when attempting to reduce operator movement. Challenge every aspect of the production process, and think of creative ways to limit hand and foot movement.

When you read about the Flow and Pull concepts later, you will appreciate the advantage of limiting people and material movement. A few seconds saved can result in balanced processes that have predictable and attainable results.

Groups of People in Downstream Processes waiting for the Completion of upstream work

The upstream supplier in this example of waste can be either an outside supplier or an internal upstream department. In some production facilities, seeing departments idle during a workday is not uncommon.

The waiting is caused by an upstream supplier who was not able to meet the material requirement of the downstream process.

There are many reasons for an external or internal supplier being late with a delivery.

- Your schedule is unstable and requires constant changes

- Shortages in the particular commodity that you use

- Machine breakdowns

- Strikes or slowdowns at supplier or transportation companies

- Unrealistic supplier lead times

- MRP systems with inaccurate databases

- Poor scheduling

- Poor attendance

- Processes that cannot yield the required amounts in the required time intervals

- Parts, or assemblies, that do not meet the required specifications

- Parts, or assemblies, cannot be located

There are numerous other reasons why downstream operations may become idle. It is your job to challenge each situation as it arises, and create a way to limit your exposure.

Administrative processes are loaded with activities that assure that operations move at a slow pace. As an example, many people have to wait for a review and approval routine to take place before a task can be completed and the documents requiring review and approval are usually batch processed. The typical Engineering Change Notice (ECN) process that usually has multiple review and approval routines before a change can be implemented is a specific example.

At one client location the ECN process took an average of eighty-two days to complete. The average was determined by examining ECN documentation for a period of three years. When the ECN process was examined in detail, it was determined that the value-added time associated with the process was approximately thirteen hours. This ECN process will be discussed in more detail later in this book.

Mostly every company will have an approval matrix for just about every activity that is performed. This is partly the reason that many people wait for an upstream process to work before they can get their job done. Control systems that bring administrative processes to a virtual halt must be challenged, and methods to reduce the human interactivity should be provided, while maintaining the *necessary* controls.

Producing Goods or Services that do not meet the Specific Needs of Customers

A good example of this type of waste is the company that rushes to release a new product. In the attempt to be first to market, the product does not meet the exact needs of the customer, and the anticipated orders do not materialize or are less frequent. The company is stuck with inventory that will not move from the shelf, or has to rework the material (if possible) before it can be sold.

Lean Enterprise requires that you spend the time to determine the value for each product. This should not be perceived value. You should take the time to make sure that your product meets the needs of your prospective customer base. The process that you use to deliver this value will also determine if you have a customer for your products. Even if your product meets the specifications of your customers, a costly or untimely process will limit your success on price and delivery alone. Over-engineering is another example of producing goods that do not meet the specific needs of your customer. Customers will not want to purchase your products if a competitor is providing a model that has the capability and price that meets their needs. Offering products with bells and whistles that add no value to a customer's product, service, or process will not always work.

Companies can get caught-up in chasing perceived value. Sales and marketing personnel sometimes attempt to take the place of customers and want to direct the R&D or product design engineering effort. The desires of a limited number of customers are frequently mistaken as being capabilities that all customers would value.

Taking shortcuts in the production process to cut costs, or to meet production goals, is another example of a manufacturing miscalculation that creates unhappy customers and usually results in product returns.

Failure to Fully Utilize the Time and Talents of People

The attitude in many companies is that it is not possible for production workers or lower-level administrators to grasp creative concepts for change. They hire expensive executive talent and expect that any change in the way they do business will come from this pool. This "check your brain at the door" mentality is the reason why many improvement programs fail.

In one Fortune 500 company where we attempted to sell our interactive Lean educational software, management could not see how they could leverage our program that was created to train every employee in the company. With the focus on their high-level management staff and project-oriented program, the company did not believe that line employees could contribute to the resolution of the problems that they had. This company has been involved in a Lean transformation for several years, and by any expert standards has failed.

Why is it that production workers that are talented enough to run their own households on limited budgets and can probably repair any appliance or piece of machinery that they own, are perceived by managers as not having the ability to contribute to an improvement process? It is our experience that those workers are very capable and can contribute very creative ideas to solve problems when they have been given the opportunity to do so.

We could write a book on this subject alone. If you attempt a Lean transformation, and do not involve everyone in your company, you will fail! You must educate everyone in your company and implement Lean concepts via Kaizen teams consisting of employees from all levels, and all disciplines.

Kaizen

A Kaizen is a three-to five-day event intended to examine and make improvements to current processes while meeting the goals that management establishes as the organization strives to be Lean. The length of time necessary for the event is dependent on the complexity of the process. Do not allow Kaizen events to exceed five days and be sure that the results are presented to management on the final day of the event.

The Kaizen team is comprised of at least one person who is familiar with the process being examined, along with four or five other individuals. The size of the team should be based on the complexity and nature of the process, as well as the number of departments in the company that may be involved. It is very important that at least half of the participants on the Kaizen team be from other departments. They can step outside the box and think of a creative way to perform a process step. If multiple shifts are involved, be sure to include representatives from the additional shifts in the event.

While management can, and should, participate in the initial training for the Kaizen event, their influence over the Kaizen should stop there. Actual participation by management in the Kaizen can interfere with the creative thinking process that you want to occur, and can inhibit a good result. If managers participate in a Kaizen event, they must do so as a member of the team. For the purpose of that event, they have no authority or management privilege.

The basic job of the Kaizen team is to document the current process and make the necessary changes in that process to meet the Lean goals established by management.

If you have studied group behavior, you can expect that everything you learned can (and likely will) occur during a Kaizen event. We have overseen Kaizens where nothing was accomplished for the first two days. We would walk into the room and hear participants going at each other in their attempt to influence the outcome, or to establish their role on the team. Eventually, calmer heads would prevail, and someone in the group would remind everyone else that the deadline for the completion of the project was nearing, and that they needed to get something done. This is usually when the team organized itself into smaller groups that were responsible for separate elements, and began to get some work done. As you progress through the Lean implementation, this aspect of group behavior should become less of an issue.

As the facilitator of a Kaizen event, you must make sure that the process flow that is developed to depict the current process is accurate. To do this, you may want to verify certain portions, or the entire process, prior to continuing with the event. A lot of time can be wasted if the process is not understood by all. The more detailed the team gets with the process flow, and the more accurately they calculate the time taken to perform that process, the better. If the up-front flow of the current process is done correctly, it is almost impossible not to show dramatic improvements once the Kaizen event is completed and the new process is in place.

You must act upon the improvements that are created. The purpose of the Kaizen event is to change the process, not to create a to-do list for improvements and have a management team decide on the merits of those improvements. You present to management the detailed flow, and timeline of the old process, and then take them through the new process. You may want to bring the management team to the actual process to demonstrate the new capability.

While we have never participated in, or facilitated, a Kaizen event that did not improve the process, we have seen Kaizen events that did not meet all of the goals established. If this happens to you, it is not a cause for alarm. It likely means that you tried to bite-off more than you could chew. Praise the participants for what they were able to accomplish, and have them continue the event to complete the project. Celebrate any and all results. Kaizen events should always end with a presentation to management by the entire team. Regardless of the level of participation by each member of the team, they should all be a part of the final presentation. After a while, you will discover that you have some pretty competent presenters at every level in your organization. If you have team members who are terrified of speaking in public, do not force the issue; rather, have them participate in the presentation in some other way. A question and answer session may be more appropriate for those individuals. Remember: management does not expect a professional presentation: however, they do expect professional results.

In one plant in our prior company, visitors who wished to view the plant operation were first given a presentation of the Lean program by line personnel. Plant management did not participate in this presentation and the individuals assigned to the presentation were usually given very short notice to prepare the presentations were flawless and always brought praise from the visitors.

As a final note regarding the Kaizen event, no one team member is more important than any other. The focus for the entire three to five days must be the event itself. For the period of the event, no one has anything more important to do. If one person takes a break, everybody takes a break. The facilitator of the event is responsible for setting the rules, and making sure that everyone understands that they have been committed to the project.

The Five Elements of Lean

There are five elements of Lean; Value, Value Stream, Flow, Pull, and Perfection.

Value

In this context, we are describing Value as perceived by the customer. There is only one way to determine what value means to the customer: you ask. The customer, when speaking in Lean Enterprise terms, is any person, process, or organization that is downstream of an activity. This means, for example, that final assembly within the manufacturing process is the customer of upstream sub-assembly departments. Value to final assembly is a kit of quality parts delivered on time to meet the demand placed on them by the end customer. Value to the final assembly department is also an order that clearly defines and meets the request of the customer. Value should be determined for each product or service offered by your company.

As we have said, it is not unusual that companies find themselves chasing value because each salesperson is sure that they know what the customer wants. In reality, what is being presented is what the salesperson and his or her customer agreed to; if you want that business, then you will have to meet the contract expectations. From that point on, your margins start to deteriorate and you will be fortunate to make it through the exercise and make a profit. It's almost as if the salesperson and your customer form an alliance, and then they attack.

It is vital that sales and marketing personnel learn Lean concepts and participate in the Lean transformation. Value selling must accompany the Lean transformation. As you have probably learned from dealing with your own suppliers, quality is the ultimate requirement. Where low-cost material is the only consideration, it can lead to major problems. Your customers should be sold on the value of your product and the efficiency of your processes. If your organization provides outstanding customer service, and the product works as designed every time and can be delivered on time and in the proper quantities,then price can be a secondary consideration.

Try to think of the products that you have purchased in the past where price was not the primary consideration. You wanted the product to work as it was intended every time you used it. It is not uncommon to realize, well after your purchase, that the lowest price does not necessarily mean lowest total cost.

Determining value, and making a value statement is critical to the success of the follow-on processes of becoming Lean. A lot of work can be wasted, and projects can fail, if value was misunderstood, or was not determined by direct inquiry from the customer. We can't stress enough the importance of this step. We would not attempt to define value in a company until senior management and key line management personnel had received extensive training on Lean concepts, and had committed to implement and participate in the Lean Enterprise transformation. Recognizing that prior concepts of value have been distorted and are wasteful is a milestone for management. Attempting or continuing a Lean implementation without this understanding will not bear fruit. As we explore Lean further, the importance of inter-departmental participation in defining and creating value will be discussed.

Meeting the value requirement is not necessarily associated with the effort expended. I (Keith Gilpatrick) am a sixty-year-old man who is somewhat of a physical fitness freak. No, I'm not one of those old men that appear to be stumbling down the road early in the day. I limit my fitness regime to working with weights at the neighborhood fitness

Value Flow

Enterprise Level

Downstream Flow

Supplier – Receiving – Incoming Inspection – Manufacturing – Shipping – Customer

Upstream Flow

Customer – Shipping – Manufacturing – Incoming Inspection – Receiving – Supplier

Operations Level

Downstream Flow

Planning Scheduling – Purchasing – Supplier – Receiving – Warehouse

Sub-assembly Process A, B, C, D, etc. – Warehouse – Final Assembly

Warehouse – Order Entry – Warehouse – Shipping – Customer

Upstream Flow

Customer – Shipping – Warehouse – Order Entry – Warehouse – Final

Assembly – Warehouse – Sub-assembly Process A, B, C, D, etc. – Warehouse

Receiving – Supplier – Purchasing – Planning Scheduling

center. While I have been working out three times a week for longer than I care to remember, I've got to tell you that my success with that program is only about one year old. I was like a lot of people in the fitness center who appear to be working-out but do not manage to accomplish much. It was not for a lack of effort. I would spend almost two hours each day working out. After an honest evaluation of what I was actually doing, I determined that I was making two mistakes. I was using too much weight, and my methods (posture, for example) were not correct. Once I reduced the amount of weight and concentrated on methods, I began to notice that I was getting stronger and that my appearance was changing.

The point I wish to make is that it can look and feel like you are doing something called exercise but if you don't do it correctly, and with the right amount of weight, you will not be happy with the results. The Lean transformation is the same. If you do not understand the various steps, or do not perform them properly, it will look like you are becoming Lean but you will not get the value results that you desire.

You should continually appraise value. At a Kaizen event at a water meter plant in the United States, we were attempting to balance a production line to determine the correct staffing levels and to increase the line's productivity. It was determined that the pace of the manufacturing process was dictated by test time. As can happen in a Kaizen event, someone not familiar with testing asked why a water meter would require such precise testing; suggesting that it would be different if the meter was measuring the flow of oil. Following the principle that no question is a dumb question, we investigated the actual regulatory requirements for water meters and were surprised to note that the actual testing requirements were somewhat less than those being performed. Years ago, someone in marketing had the idea to exceed the regulatory testing requirements, and promote that fact in hope that it would attract business. This was an internal value decision that added costs to the product, and increased the production time, but did little to provide a competitive advantage for the company in the long term.

While we continued on with the Kaizen event, and balanced the line to the current requirements, one of the action items resulting from the event was to investigate the actual savings in production time that could be gained if the plant returned to a test that met the requirement of the standard. As you will learn later when we discuss Flow, seconds saved in a process can be quite meaningful. Determining value has a significant impact on what is produced, how it is produced, and the cost of production.

Value Stream

If you manage to define value (this could be a moving target as you work with your customer to define their wants), you will need to present how value is delivered for each product that you manufacture or each service that you provide. The best way to do this is to prepare a value stream flowchart (map).

You must identify and present each step taken by your customer, you, and your suppliers in delivering the product or service. This is critical, and should have the participation of the people who know those steps best. As you start the change process, it is very important for you to make sure that the process flow that you prepare is a true representation of the facts. It is not uncommon to find that management, and others involved in the process, have lost contact with that process, and that they may not be aware of what is actually being done. A timeline must be included in the value stream process flow as well as an indication of who (department, process, vendor, etc.) is involved in each step. At the end of the value stream mapping process, you should have identified and presented each step taken, who performs each step, the information and paperwork flow, what IT systems are used, and how long the process takes.

The astounding result of most value stream maps is that there is a significant difference between the lead time for the product and the actual value added time to manufacture the product. Your goal in becoming a Lean provider is to eliminate as much of the non-value added activity as possible.

Having stressed the importance of defining and flowing value, we have to tell you that only one plant in our former company ever did value stream mapping. This is another reason why they were never completely successful in their Lean implementation. Management was so focused on the immediate savings and performance improvements that could be gained by Flow and Pull that they did not want to take the time to consider value and the value stream. What resulted were plants that looked Lean but, in fact, were not.

Most customers want products or services delivered on time, in specific quantities, at the highest quality, and at a competitive price. Establishing Flow and Pull systems alone will not always meet those customer needs. Focusing on two of the five elements will not guarantee success. Additionally, Lean Enterprise is exactly what the term suggests – it is the entire enterprise that has to be improved. Focusing on manufacturing alone will not get the job done.

This is not to suggest that you cannot begin training and implementing Flow and Pull systems within your operation immediately. What we are suggesting is that everyone in your company be trained on Lean Enterprise philosophy and techniques so that the entire enterprise will be improved as you progress. We would also encourage the training of suppliers and customers early in your journey.

When examining the current process, you must consider each process step and determine if there is any value in continuing to perform those steps.

- Value Added (VA) activity is activity that must be performed to provide products and services that match the expectations of your customers (such as assembling products).

- Non-Value-Added (NVA) activity is any activity that does not add value to your products or services (such as multiple approval signatures, incoming inspection, and inspection)

- Non-Value-Added Required (NVAR) activity is effort expended to perform activities that have no value but are required (such as cycle counting, certain inspection procedures, excessive movement of material, and excessive people movement)

Once you are satisfied that value has been defined, and you have correctly presented the flow of value in your company, you need to put a program in place that will eliminate the NVA effort immediately and plan improvements that will eventually eliminate the NVAR effort. Doing this will result in processes with little or no waste, greatly improved throughput times, fewer people, more meaningful information systems, and less documentation. Additionally, people will begin to feel that management will not accept waste in any form, and that a new culture is being formed in which they are allowed to participate. It is not unusual for some levels of management to feel threatened by their removal from certain approval processes. This is one of the more difficult aspects of the Lean transformation. Management needs to understand that they are expected to create change and provide processes that add value. To do this, the company needs to trust employees, and not waste time and resources with activities that are contrary to the value-added principle.

Flow

Flow is the processing of one piece at a time throughout the entire process and is commonly referred to as "one-piece-flow" or "single-piece-flow." In the office, we have termed this "one-need-flow: This is easy to say but is an aspect of Lean Enterprise that is greeted with much argument. Some veterans of the current batch or mass production process will argue that producing in batches is faster and more efficient. The batch processing mentality is deeply rooted in our lives and is difficult to defeat. The primary reason for this thinking is that we were brought-up thinking about doing things in batches.

Laundry is a good example of this batch mentality. Our parents have always done laundry in batches, and we can see no other way to do this. Why? Because washing machines are so large that it would be a waste to wash just one item. You could wash what you wore today, and wear the same clothes tomorrow except that all your friends would frown upon this, and you would become a social outcast. It is not that it is not possible; it is that it is not acceptable. The washing machine was in invented to make our lives easier. At the same time it has created a society that has closets full of clothes and that is not likely to accept seeing you in the same clothes you wore yesterday. Additionally, no piece of clothing is made today that would withstand daily washing and last very long. Try to think of other things that you do in batches, and identify the reasons why. In most cases, single piece processing will be possible but there will be some social, economic, or other perceived reason why it is not done. You batch your laundry, bills, errands, food preparation, letters, etc., for any number of reasons.

In manufacturing, for example, you could be batch processing electronic components because one process step is curing an adhesive or compound that must be done in large ovens. In Lean, this process would be called a "curtain operation." The only way to eliminate the batch processing is to find an adhesive, or compound, that cures faster, or find an oven that is smaller, and can cure faster. Alternatively, you can find a way to eliminate the need for curing completely. We will return to the subject of "curtain operations" later. For now, we simply wanted to identify a batch process that has been created and accepted for reasons that were not viewed as correctable or simply as the best way to get the job done. Analyzing "curtain operations" is a very interesting aspect of the transformation from batch processing to single piece flow, and can produce large savings in machinery and labor, and improved throughput times.

Most plants have been organized to facilitate batch processing. Let's look at an imaginary plant that manufactures an item that has a combination of metal, plastic, glass, wire, and electronics. Some of these are made in the plant and some are purchased from outside vendors. If the plant manufactures the metal parts, there are likely to be many parts of different sizes and different types of metal. Some of the other parts may require some sub-assembly before they can be sent to a final assembly area. Traditional mass-manufacturing thinking would have the plant organized into departments that batch process the various parts in separate areas of the plant. These parts would be manufactured on an assembly schedule that would create a large inventory of individual parts and sub-assemblies that would be used later in the final assembly department. The final assembly department would build finished parts that would be inventoried to meet a forecasted need.

So, envision the typical mass-manufacturing plant with a raw material warehouse and separate departments that manufacture parts to be used in the finished product. Additionally, there is a finished goods warehouse that houses all of the finished goods that do not have an immediate customer need. The plant could, and most likely does, have separate areas for the various processes separated by walls and large distances between each process. Looking at this plant you would see pallets of parts, and finished goods, stored throughout, waiting for someone to take them to the next step in the process. You would likely see a lot of people, and equipment, moving about the plant transferring material, sub-assemblies, and finished goods to various areas of the facility. You may even see conveyor belts throughout the plant that were installed to facilitate the hands-free movement of material. These conveyor belts are likely to be filled with parts or products waiting for someone to take them off for use in the next process. To the Lean thinker, who aspires to single piece flow, this imaginary plant is a real nightmare. The Lean person would consider much of the activity as both waste and opportunity as follows:

- The separate areas for manufacturing, sub-assembly, and final assembly, and the distance between them represents potential savings in floor space which could be used to manufacture other products, or forgo the need, and cost necessary, to build additional manufacturing space.

- More people than are necessary are being used to support the current requirements of the plant.

- Few of the people visible are adding value to the product.

- The costs of holding the raw material, work-in-process, and inventory that is present in the facility could be significantly reduced.

- Equipment may be oversized and not appropriate to meet the actual production requirement of the plant. Quick-change techniques would allow the plant to manufacture only in quantities that are necessary to meet current needs.

- There may be opportunities to provide a clean and safe environment for workers.

- People performing non-value-added activities are a resource for the transformation from batch processing to single-piece flow.

- Opportunities exist to save money by implementing total productive maintenance programs to extend the life of equipment and prevent costly breakdowns that inhibit Flow and interfere with the on-time delivery of products.

- There is an opportunity to visually present the goals of the plant, and to show how well everyone in the plant is working to meet those goals.

- A tremendous opportunity exists to save substantial cost and create additional business by being the best manufacturer of that product.

The Lean thinker would also have seen other areas of the plant where support groups like accounting, production engineering, research and development, sales, customer service, quality control, purchasing, scheduling, production control, shipping and receiving, etc., are working. He or she would see batch processing throughout these departments as well. The Lean person would hear employees talking amongst each other, and also to customers, saying that they would have to get back to them at a later time with the answer. He or she would see or hear evidence of expediting of material or customer deliveries. He or she would see empty desks or people walking around with lots of paperwork in their hands. He or she would see piles of paper and rows of file cabinets, approval stamps, voucher stamps, reports, policy manuals, conference rooms or offices with people in them discussing the problem or project of the day. Basically it's the same scene as was witnessed in the plant; batch processing with a lot of people visible who are not adding value. The Lean thinker sees a lot of opportunities to add value, speed the process up, and eliminate costs by implementing Lean concepts within those departments.

As we get into more detail about one-piece flow you should be able to see how this concept can be applied to administrative functions. So, how would our Lean thinker go about transforming this imaginary plant from a batch processor to single-piece flow? To start with, the Lean person would have needed to define the value stream for each product manufactured. Having done this, that person would know exactly what equipment is used to make each product, who operates that equipment, where that equipment is located, and how the various materials that are used to manufacture the product move through the plant.

Armed with this knowledge, equipment, people and processes can be organized to manufacture and assemble each finished product using a single-piece flow system. Some Lean gurus like to establish focused factories where there are separate production areas or mini factories within a factory. You've probably already asked yourself how a company would do this if certain items of equipment are needed to support all or more than one product. Well, you don't need to go out and buy more equipment. Using the next element of Lean Enterprise, the pull system combined with quick-change techniques, you can accommodate this situation and you can reach one-piece flow without establishing large work-in-process inventories, or purchasing more costly equipment. Let's get back to our Lean person who will transform a batch process into a Lean one-piece flow process. The first thing that should be done is to establish a Kaizen team to plan and execute the transition. The goal presented to the team should be to manufacture a quality finished product one piece at a time, eliminating as much people and inventory movement as possible. The goal should also include the reduction of work-in-process to equal, or come as close as possible to, the number of production steps in the process. For example, if there are ten machines and ten people assembling the sub-assemblies and final product, you should attempt to get WIP inventory to fewer than twenty items. If you have curtain operations within your production process, you may have more WIP inventory around until you can improve or eliminate those operations.

Do not let walls get in the way of your goal to eliminate, or reduce, the distance people and inventory move in the process. To the extent that it is feasible, move equipment and create a cell for the product being manufactured. The cost of removing a wall or moving a machine will be absorbed by the savings in process time, and the payroll saved by not requiring material handling. We have conducted Kaizen events where whole new lines were developed in completely different parts of the plant that saved huge amounts of space. This is usually accomplished comfortably within the timeframe of the Kaizen event, and costs a little overtime on the part of your maintenance crew. We have changed water and airline connections, and changed the direction of the flow of a process many times. Done within the confines of the Kaizen event, this process takes the place of traditional work order requests that can take weeks to be created and implemented. (Just do it!) If there is equipment that serves several production cells, move that equipment as close as possible to those cells. Then create a Kanban signal system that delivers just enough inventory to meet the current needs of each production cell.

An important goal of the Kaizen team will be to balance the work necessary to produce the finished product so that each machine, and individual, in the process is taking approximately the same amount of time to complete the work. This is referred to as Line Balancing. When viewed on a single-piece flow basis, it will be obvious that certain machines, or people, have made (more or less) time to accomplish their processes than others in the line. This can be easily understood when you consider that a machine that stamps a metal part for the finished product does so in a three or four-second cycle compared to a person who might take 30 seconds to assemble that same part into the product. The bottom line is that no part of the process should be working any faster than the slowest part of the process, otherwise inventory will build up between the steps. This is another area of Lean that causes concern. People have difficulty getting used to the idea that large stamping machines that can produce thirty or more parts a minute should be slowed down to produce only one every thirty seconds. If a machine can be dedicated to a cell it should in fact be slowed to produce only what is needed when it is needed. However, when the large machine is used to supply more than one line, the production must be planned so that each line has only the amount required for production. This can be accomplished with a well planned Kanban system for those lines and a quick change program for the equipment. In a "greenfield" situation, where you are setting up a new line or plant to produce a new product, you should consider down-sizing equipment to meet the needs of the new process.

A good example of this situation was presented to us when one of our client companies had a process that required parts to be shipped to an outside processor for heat treatment. This resulted in a need to purchase or produce large batches of parts in order to provide the vendor with quantities that would be 'economical' for him to heat treat. This produced two negative situations. Firstly, we were required to produce large batches in advance of the actual requirement. The second was that the heat treatment was not consistent, and the quality of the returned parts was poor. This was solved after our Six-Sigma black belt determined that the problem was caused by the vendor because they were heat treating several different parts together, and that the process did not heat treat evenly. Our solution was to design a machine that would heat treat one piece at a time and do it evenly at a speed that matched demand. The result was a huge reduction in inventory. This ultimately paid for the new machines when you amortized the costs of carrying the inventory against the cost of the new machines over their expected useful lives. Another significant benefit was that we were in control of the process.

Another example was a plant that manufactured small motors. They were required to lacquer the copper windings of those motors prior to final assembly. Using the old system, the copper windings were dipped in a lacquer and hung on an overhead conveyor that covered a major portion of the plant and traveled for several hours to dry. While the windings came off the conveyor at a speed that matched final assembly, there was a tremendous amount of inventory traveling around the plant drying. The creative solution to this problem was to design a machine that would hold one winded motor at a time and spin dry the winding in seconds. The result was that hundreds of winded motors were taken from the WIP inventory, and a copper winded motor part was available at the speed of the process. The savings were significant. You can imagine how much better the employees felt not being exposed to the odor of lacquered parts passing over their heads. Furthermore, the OSHA problems created by the old system and the high costs to maintain that process were eliminated.

When you are performing the Line Balancing technique, it is helpful to know just how fast the line should be working in order to provide product at the rate it is needed. There are two ways to approach this. All of the books on Lean discuss Takt Time. Takt Time is the time it should take to build an item of finished goods to meet the needs of your customer. Simply stated, you divide the quantities that your customer needs over a specific period of time into the time available in your plant to manufacture during that same time period. To do this, convert the time available into seconds and divide the resulting number by the total demand of your customers for that same time. An example of a Takt Time calculation is presented in the Tools section of this chapter. The visual presentation of Takt Time is shown on the Line Balance chart, also presented in the Tools section.

As a second option, let's assume that you have a backlog that is causing poor customer relations, and you are not in a competitive position within your industry. In this situation, you would disregard Takt Time, and focus on improving your processes, and balancing your production lines to maximize your production rate. Once you have eliminated your backlog, and have determined what actual Takt Time should be for any period, you should rebalance your lines, or limit the hours of production to meet the actual Takt Time.

Another option for a production line that has been operating in a balanced fashion at a maximum rate is to introduce a rabbit chase process. Using a rabbit chase, you would take a certain number of people out of the balanced line, and have the remaining people walk a product through the entire process. Using this method you can vary the rate of production when demand declines. You should strive to meet Takt Time, but there can be advantages to using the alternatives.

Balancing work is a technique that also applies to administrative processes. If you take a good look around your office you will see people who appear to have time to talk, and do other non-work related activities, while others have their heads down and are very busy. Balancing work in your office can have a wide range of benefits. While some people might not like being busy all the time, those who already are will relish the fact that some of their burden is being relieved.

Pull

The Pull element involves the continuous flow of parts and assemblies through the entire production process in quantities, and at a rate, demanded by the downstream customer. Basically, if there is no demand for the product, or if the demand slows, then the production line stops or slows down to meet the need. Pull starts at final assembly when a customer order is received, and ends at your supplier location. Pull is accomplished through the use of a Kanban signal that represents an order from a downstream process to an upstream supplier for a specific quantity of quality parts, or material, to be delivered at an agreed upon time. You will only order from an upstream supplier when there is a signal indicating real demand. It is possible when you combine Pull and Kanban concepts to have a paperless production process. Implementing Pull in your manufacturing process can significantly reduce all classes of inventory. We have seen many cases where WIP inventory reductions have exceeded ninety percent. Making the transition from a Material Requirements Planning (MRP) based production process to a Pull process will require an aggressive value selling effort. You will want your customers to order only what they need for the short term. You need to commit to the timely production and shipment of customer orders that are smaller and received at a faster pace. Customers need to understand the costs that they incur when ordering product for which there is no immediate need. If your customer is using MRP, they have the same inventory build-up problems because MRP relies on sales forecasts and has safety stock provisions that create inventory before there is a real need.

Many companies have attempted the Pull system. They have done so under the name of Just-In-Time (JIT). Well in advance of the introduction of Lean concepts, consultants devised improvement programs targeting inventory investment using the leverage large companies had over suppliers to implement the JIT concept. The problem with JIT is that it does not work well as a standalone concept. Incorporating JIT (Kanban) and the remaining elements of Lean is much more effective.

Perfection

Perfection is constantly striving to streamline all processes to eliminate waste. It is becoming the very best at everything you do. Once you have identified Value and completed your initial Value Stream Mapping exercises, you must continue to refine these processes so that they become the very best solution to deliver that Value. Accepting anything other than absolute perfection is counter to Lean. This is the key to the culture change that must take place in your company. Each employee must adopt the attitude that the process they work on will be the best, and they should expect that others in the enterprise will have the same attitude. Employees should have no fear of recommending improvements to upstream suppliers of products or services.

The focus of Lean must remain on value and the processes that deliver value. You can not discriminate in your implementation of Lean. For many, it is tempting to go after the low-hanging fruit that results from the Flow element of Lean. The early savings that can be attained by balancing the production processes can be impressive. However, any attempt to place the focus solely on the production process will limit your success. Not only are you missing a major opportunity, but only a few in your organization will believe that the Lean concepts apply to them. The fact is that most employees know the processes are broken. They will view a production-only process improvement initiative as the "program of the month" and they will believe that management is not committed to Lean.

The Four Rules of Lean

Several years after publication of *Lean Thinking*, the *Harvard Business Review* published the results of a study performed by Steven Spear and Kent Bowen which focused on the reasons why Toyota had success with the Toyota Production System and why not all of the companies that attempted Lean transformations experienced the same success. The title of this article was "Decoding the DNA of the Toyota Production System."[3]

Our interpretation of the *Harvard Business Review* study was that Toyota had four rules that they followed religiously.

- Standard Work - Develop processes that are free of waste, documented, and repeatable.

- Limit the distance material travels within the process.

- Limit People Movement - both hand and foot.

- Educate to the lowest level in the organization.

We believe these rules further our argument that Lean is a process improvement methodology. These rules must be applied to everything that is done in your business. When you compare the product lead time to the actual value added time performed by direct manufacturing labor personnel you will understand that there is significantly more time spent administering the business than there is manufacturing product.

As Lean practitioners, we are constantly confronted with cumbersome, or faulty, production processes that can be corrected easily by following the rules of Lean.

---

[3] *Spear, Steven and Bowen, Kent. "Decoding the DNA of the Toyota Production System."* Harvard Business Review. Boston: 1999.

"

Standard Work

When developing or performing any process, you must ensure that the process adds value, is repeatable, is documented, and that everyone performing the process is following a standard that will create the desired result.

Earlier, we introduced the Albert Einstein quote "To repeat the same thing over and over and expect that the results will change is insanity." We use this quote early in our introduction to Lean to make the point that management cannot expect different results if they do not change the way they do business. (See Chapter 2 – 'The Need for Change.') The quote also applies in reverse: if you create a process that is repeatable, the results will not change (Standard Work).

One focus of Six-Sigma is the identification and elimination of process variations. Lean can also eliminate a lot of quality problems that result from process variations by implementing Standard Work. Companies can limit their exposure to scrap and rework costs by combining Standard Work with the concepts of Flow.

As Lean consultants, we frequently run into situations where production managers have lost touch with the process and fail to recognize that variations in assembly technique have evolved. The assembly lines experience sporadic quality issues. This is common fare in the non-Lean production facility. Variations are accepted as inevitable by managers and supervisors. When variations are encountered, they are corrected and production continues unabated until another variation occurs.

The problem with this method of managing production is that the root cause of the errors is rarely found by anyone in the immediate process, and the cost of the error is multiplied as the product moves through the process. The worst-case scenario is that the customer cannot use the product as it was produced.

Standard-work is meant to combat the reactive style of production management. A good standard will incorporate self-inspection prior to passing a processed part or assembly downstream. A Lean production supervisor or manager will focus on the process (and methods) to limit process variations. After a very short period of time, employees will adopt a sense of quality ownership and will follow the standards, or will recommend a change if one is necessary. People will also be more aware of the quality provided by the upstream supplier. They will ensure that the part that they are about to process meets the standard for that part, and will stop processing if and when a problem is noticed. Deploying Standard Work should have a significant positive impact on your cost of quality. Scrap costs and rework activity should be reduced, if not completely eliminated.

Limiting Material/Information Travel

The distance between upstream and downstream processes must be minimized. Traditional mass-manufacturing processes resulted in large plants with great distances between processes. This distance was necessary because of the large Work-In-Process (WIP) inventories that were produced by machines or production workers because production was not balanced to the speed and actual demand of the end customer. Production used MRP systems that planned production based on actual backlog plus forecasted sales. This was coupled with a mentality that every process should be at 100% productivity.

Combining this rule with the Flow and Pull elements of Lean will provide astounding results. If the distance between upstream and downstream processes does not allow for a direct pass of product through the process, you are likely to have a process that is wasteful.

In a typical mass-manufacturing plant, forklift trucks are plentiful. The plant will have wide aisles throughout to accommodate the forklift traffic. It is not unusual to see that all material travels through a plant on pallets. A process will receive a pallet of material, empty that pallet, process the material, and load another pallet which will be moved to the next downstream process. In a plant such as this, there are usually many pallets waiting to be moved to the next downstream process, or back to a warehouse for storage. There is a huge amount of material travel, sometimes miles, before raw material is transformed into finished goods.

There are Lean people who do not advocate the use of conveyor systems for the movement of material. This use of conveyors is discouraged because conveyors frequently become material storage areas for parts, and assemblies that are waiting for further processing. We have some empathy with this approach. However, we do not discourage the use of conveyors if they are short, and operate on a gate or limit switch system that prevents the buildup of parts, or assemblies.

Limiting People Hand/Feet Travel

When you attempt to introduce Flow and Pull into your manufacturing processes, you will understand the importance of limiting people movement. When you manufacture at the demand of your downstream customer (Takt Time), limiting people movement is a must. We will expand on Takt Time later, and the significance of saving seconds by limiting people hand/feet movement will become clearer. Excess movement is usually caused by a poor plant layout. Things are never where they need to be. In a typical non-Lean plant, you will notice a lot of movement by employees. They are either walking around looking for something that they need to get their job done, or the layout of materials that they use to produce parts, assemblies, or finished goods is not as good as it could be. Every time a worker has to walk a long distance or reach excessively there is an opportunity for error.

The variations involved in operator movement can be the cause of poor quality. Injuries are more likely when you have workers making awkward movements, or when they are in areas that they should not be in looking for parts, tools, or cleaning materials.

You will be surprised at the increase in process speed that can be achieved by focusing on this rule of Lean. Keep in mind, however, that no single process step should operate any faster than it needs to operate in order to meet the demand of the downstream customer. Simply going for speed can result in an unbalanced process that will result in the buildup of inventory between processes.

Later, we will present the 5S tool which focuses on a clean and well organized plant. 5S should be one of the first Lean initiatives in your Lean transformation. Your plant needs to be as clean as you can make it and everything used to produce products, adjust machinery, repair machinery, or clean the work area must be available for ease of use. Again, the primary focus is on movement.

One exception to the movement rule is a Rabbit Chase process where each worker walks through the entire process performing all the process steps that are required to produce a finished item or sub-assembly. While this concept appears to contradict the limited movement rule, the Rabbit Chase process is an appropriate means of matching production with non-linear demand. The Rabbit Chase concept is explained in more detail in the Tools section.

Educate to the Lowest Level in the Organization

This is the most important rule. Your success in implementing Lean will be based, in large part, on your willingness, and ability, to provide a Lean education to every employee in your company. This must be done as quickly as possible. A slow introduction of Lean concepts, or limiting the education to a few, will have negative consequences. Educating slowly will not provide the momentum needed to attain dramatic change, and limiting the participation will bring the program to its knees through overload or burnout. Every employee needs to know what Lean is about, and the program needs to be fueled by those employees who grasp the concepts and force rapid and continuing change.

We are constantly confronted with cross-functional issues when we are attempting to sell our educational software to companies who are considering or are currently engaged in a Lean transformation. Many companies are locked into the classroom training mentality, and wrestle with the e-learning concept. Few companies are equipped for e-learning, despite the major cost and scheduling advantages. Production operators do not often have access to computers, and few companies promote "learn on your own time" programs for salaried employees.

We have a client who purchased our educational software and gave each salaried employee a deadline for completion of their Lean education. Within three months this client had more Lean activities underway than any other client we have worked with. The CEO recognized the value of a swift education followed by engagement. Within six months, there were employees at all levels involved in self-directed improvement programs. The Lean Champion used to have to beg supervisors to allow people to participate in Kaizen events. After the education program began, he spent much of his time recording the results of Kaizen events that were being held. The Lean Champion became the Lean Administrator and others in the company assumed the Facilitator responsibilities.

Several years after James Womack introduced Lean concepts, he and his associates at the Lean Enterprise Institute concluded that one of the primary reasons why Lean was not as successful as it could be was the lack of a good Lean education program. Most of the companies that they contacted had very structured programs that did not include educating everyone in the company.

One great student at Akron University Lean Mastery's Program was a CNC machine operator from a company that produced intricate metal parts. This young man quickly grasped the concept of waste and was able to articulate the need for Lean in almost every aspect of operations in his company. Workers like this young man are everywhere we go. When we are in plants facilitating Kaizen events, those employees who grasp the Lean concepts are the stabilizing force during the five-day event. Their enthusiasm for the program becomes contagious and people begin to focus on the project at hand.

The Tools of Lean

There are a number of tools and techniques that are used in Lean, many of which are referred to by acronyms or unusual names. This section provides a brief overview of the common Lean tools.

The Five 'S'es

5S – The basic principles of a 5S program are to create an organized, clean, and safe work area. Taken to the plant level, 5S creates a spotless plant that has excellent lighting, reduces wasted people movement, is safe, and removes everything from the plant that isn't needed.

The Five S's are Separate, Sort, Sweep, Standardize, and Sustain. (You may see different definitions in other materials; however, in essence, they all mean the same thing.)

> **Separate** – Eliminate everything that is not needed.

> **Sort** – Arrange everything in the plant, tools, parts, and machinery, so they can be accessed without wasting time and effort.

> **Sweep** – Bring the plant to a spotless condition and clean daily.

> **Standardize** – Develop procedures to assure compliance with the first three 'S's.

> **Sustain** – Maintain and improve (Kaizen) the 5S program.

5S programs can have a tremendous impact on the attitude of employees. As a general rule, once a plant or administrative work area has undergone a 5S program, the employees develop pride in their work area and seek to maintain a high level of cleanliness and organization. 5S must be introduced early in the Lean transformation to provide a signal to the employees that management is committed to Lean and dramatic changes are going to be made.

Costs that can be reduced or avoided once 5S is implemented include:

- Cost of human effort to locate tools, production materials or supplies, and documentation needed to produce products.

- Cost to replace lost tools or documentation.

- Cost to maintain a facility that is not kept clean as a standard practice.

- Cost for environmental cleanup.

- Cost to repair damaged machinery.

- Cost associated with a maintenance workforce that is larger than necessary because equipment, and facilities, are not kept clean as a standard practice.

- Cost of the excess space required to store materials, tools, and miscellaneous items that are not needed in the facility.

Any plan to implement Lean should have 5S as one of the early steps of the transformation process. Some companies we have worked with have devoted entire weekends to the 5S kickoff. Everyone in the company, including the CEO, and his or her staff, work the weekend to clean the manufacturing and administrative areas. This can be a very rewarding experience for the employees who are not accustomed to seeing senior management get their hands dirty. A good manager can get a lot of mileage out of this type of activity. They are showing people that they are not asking anyone to do something that they are not willing to do themselves.

Total Productive Maintenance (TPM)

TPM is a program for machine and tool maintenance that extends the useful life of equipment, and ensures that equipment will be available when needed to produce product. A good TPM program will include maintenance procedures for all equipment operators as well as production cell workers (Autonomous Maintenance). TPM should include scheduled preventive maintenance.

Our experience with Lean TPM initiatives has shown many instances where maintenance departments were ill prepared for such a program. Documentation critical for maintaining the machinery had been lost, or perhaps it never existed because used equipment was purchased. Production equipment maintenance records were either incomplete or inaccurate. Given the skills and experience levels of maintenance employees, certain items of equipment could not be repaired using in-house maintenance staff. Some equipment was so old that parts to repair that equipment were not currently available. There were no preventative maintenance procedures for production machinery.

A good TPM program is as vital to a successful Lean implementation as any of the Elements and Rules. The best Lean plant can come to a complete stop, and remain idle for days, if the machinery in the plant is not maintained properly. Allowing time for scheduled maintenance is critical. We have been at many plants where machines were running 24/7. Suggesting that maintenance be allowed time to perform preventive maintenance was not well received.

SMED

SMED stands for Single Minute Exchange of Dies; or, quick changeover techniques that will reduce the size of batches processed by large machines that currently have complicated and time-consuming tool and die changeover requirements. Large production machines can take several hours to change over. This is the reason why thousands of pieces are often run at one time. Enough parts are produced to supply one operation while the machine is used to make parts for others. If a machine historically takes four hours to changeover and you can cut that time to 30 minutes, you can significantly reduce the batch size production for that machine. This reduces WIP inventory by a huge amount, which can free up a lot of warehouse space.

A self-directed team, employing Kaizen concepts, performs a SMED exercise on each piece of equipment used in the production process. A successful SMED project will ultimately reduce inventory and speed up, or perhaps eliminate, traditional batch-and-queue processes. SMED concepts can also be applied to the quick changeover of production lines so that a variety of models can be produced without wasting valuable production time.

The best example of quick change at work is the racecar pit crew. Imagine how long it would take an inexperienced team to service an automobile if they did not have the proper equipment, or they were not trained to do it quickly, and did not practice these techniques regularly. The same approach used by the pit crew can be applied to machinery or production line changeovers.

We have been associated with many SMED activities where multiple teams were created to implement quick change concepts. The program would begin with an opening meeting where the teams would select a name for their team. These meetings were quite spirited, and it was not unusual that more than one team would want the Gordon, Burton, or Wallace name. Once the teams were organized, the competition to get the fastest changeover time was intense. The team members were aware of the safety and regulation issues associated with the NASCAR racing teams, and were quick to adopt their own rules regarding safety and changeover regulations.

It is virtually impossible to operate an effective Kanban system if you do not reduce batch size. You could operate a Kanban system from a warehouse that acts as the primary supplier but you will not experience the inventory reductions that are possible from balanced lines operating on a Pull system direct to the outside suppliers.

Process Mapping

Process Mapping involves the creation of process flow diagrams or charts that depict each step in a process as well as the number of people in that process and the numbers and types of documents currently used to control the process.

The process map is used to help the Kaizen team to identify value-added, non value-added, and non value-added but required steps, and to establish a time estimate for the current process.

The process map is the key to a successful Kaizen event. The facilitator of the Kaizen event must ensure that the chart for the current process is a true representation of the facts. Once the current process is accurately depicted, it serves as a basis for reporting process improvements. Process maps prepared during the Kaizen event are also used while presenting the results of the Kaizen event. If those maps are contested, it can take away from the overall team accomplishment. Wait time depicted on these maps is usually challenged, and must be supported by documented evidence. Wait time can normally be supported if there is adequate data on the documents that are a part of the system. For example, if your system calls for a management review or approval, there should be a signature block and a date signed block on the form so that the review and approval time can be calculated.

One exercise we perform during our classroom education is a team project where the team will map the process for what transpires between the time you wake up to the time you get to work. One team member is selected to define the process steps that he or she follows each day. The results of this exercise are always amusing when it is noticed that people fail to indicate process steps like switching lights and appliances on or off, or drive out of their garage without opening the doors. It is also interesting to see which process steps other team members determine to be of no value. The important message here is that process maps must depict all steps in the process and none should be omitted. This exercise has proven to be an effective early education tool. Students begin to grasp the concepts of depicting processes and evaluating the need for every process step.

Line Balancing

Line balancing is a program where each step in a production process is timed, recorded, and presented on a frequency chart with the intent to balance the work so that each process step takes about the same amount of time to complete. The purpose of Line balancing is to determine the time it takes for a single completed piece of product to be manufactured so that the rate can be compared to and matched with the actual customer demand.

To fairly and accurately depict the time taken to perform each process step you should record each process step ten times, eliminate the high and low time, and divide the total of the remaining times by eight to get an average. Once you have done this for every process step, place the results on a bar chart that also has the Takt Time shown. The results of the timing exercise will be apparent when the bar chart is complete. If any one process step takes longer than the Takt Time reflected on the bar chart, you have a process that can not meet the current customer demand.

If all process steps fall below the Takt Time line then there may be opportunities to combine process steps and have fewer people involved in the production process. Keep in mind, that in situations where multiple shifts are in operation, the line balancing exercise should include data from all shifts. Assuming that all shifts can operate at the same rate can produce disturbing results. When you time all shifts, variations in the speed of the process can surface that could not be anticipated.

A process step that takes much longer than any other is referred to as a "curtain operation." These types of steps can complicate attempts to balance a production line. A good example of a curtain operation is the curing of potting compounds. It may take several minutes for potting compounds to cure before the downstream process steps can be completed. This has caused producers to develop large machines that can process hundreds or thousands of items at the same time. Heat-treating metal parts is another example of a curtain operation. Manufacturers frequently process thousands of parts so heat-treating can be accomplished economically.

The main theory of line balancing is that the line can not operate any faster than the slowest process. This is easier to understand when you move all of the process steps close together in a production cell. When the processes are spread throughout the plant in a typical batch-and queue operation, problems are masked by the large batches of inventory. When you attempt single-piece-flow, the curtain operations and the effect they can have on attempts to balance production will become evident.

Once a curtain operation has been identified, steps must be taken to either speed up the process using different methods, or allow sufficient inventory in front of, and behind the process, to balance production. The target in establishing Flow is Takt Time. You use Takt Time to determine the rate at which the cell needs to produce in order to meet customer demand. Balancing production is critical to establishing Flow. We present an example of the Line Balancing Chart later in this chapter.

Kanban

A Kanban is a signal for demand of specific product, in specific quantities, to be delivered to a specific process. Kanban is a critical element of the Pull system. Each Kanban is sized differently to meet the replenishment requirements and capabilities of the upstream suppliers so that the downstream customer will always have adequate supply and can meet fluctuating customer demand.

The ideal Kanban system is an e-Kanban system. An electronic wand is used to indicate that a Kanban representing a specific quantity of parts has just been drawn or consumed. The signal goes directly to the upstream supplier, internal or external, where a new order is automatically processed for a replacement of the same item in the desired quantity, to be delivered within an agreed upon time span.

In a Lean plant, the final assembly department will draw upon the internal Kanban inventory once the department has received an actual customer order. When the Kanban is drawn, a signal will go immediately to the upstream supplier, and that operation will begin a process to replenish that specific amount of inventory. This process will continue through the various upstream suppliers until, eventually, an external supplier will receive a signal to replenish.

The primary difference between a Lean operation using Kanban, and a non-Lean operation attempting Just-in-Time (JIT), is that the Lean operation applies the concept throughout the enterprise on a Pull basis.

The non-Lean operation is simply working with external suppliers for a timely delivery of parts based on a scheduling system that is time sensitive, but not necessarily based on firm customer demand. Some large companies that had sufficient leverage over their suppliers have experienced some success with JIT concepts. It is possible to experience great success using Lean concepts, regardless of the size of your company, or the extent of the leverage you may have over your suppliers. Success is measured by substantial increases in inventory turns, which in turn lowers inventory carrying costs.

If you are at all nervous about using Kanban, you can include some additional Kanbans as safety stock until your upstream suppliers adjust to Kanban as a replenishment system.

Doubling annual inventory turns is a realistic goal for any company involved in a Lean transformation. Replacing your current MRP system with a Kanban system is the best way to reach an aggressive inventory turns milestone.

Poka-Yoke

Poka-Yoke is part of a broader system of error-proofing processes called Jidoka. Lean thinkers are constantly seeking ways to error-proof processes. Machines with built in stop mechanisms that prevent waste/scrap because of the mis-placement of materials or components into machines is a good example of this concept.

Your computer was manufactured with error proofing in mind. Each piece of peripheral equipment that can be attached to your computer has a connector that will only work in the appropriate slot. The primary purpose of Poka-Yoke is to prevent costly inspection and rework, and to make the end product friendly to the user.

Autonomation

This involves using man and machine to error proof a process. A typical application of this tool is the light post that you see on some production machinery. The machines are left to operate by themselves, and signal perfect operation by reflecting green, material shortage by reflecting yellow, or a material quality or machine malfunction by reflecting red. In the case of a yellow or red situation, the machine will shut itself down. Another example is the use of limit switches on machines that will not allow the machine to operate if the material is not placed correctly for accurate processing.

Poka-Yoke is an application of the Perfection element of Lean. If there are ways to eliminate process errors, they should be implemented immediately. Every Kaizen event should consider ways to error proof the process being reviewed.

Over the years we have seen some creative ways to prevent process errors. If you can create a list of everything that has gone wrong within a process or with a product, you should be able to create a corresponding list of ways to prevent those problems from repeating themselves.

It is not uncommon to see manufacturing operations that have every possible safety issue addressed relative to machines and operators. Yet, in most cases, they have done little to ensure the prevention of process errors that cause process or product quality problems.

DFMA

DFMA (Design for Manufacturing and Assembly) is a design engineering theory and the application of techniques that are used to ensure that the final design will assemble easily and will be made using fewer parts that are readily available at the best price. A good DFMA program can produce significant reductions in production time, material costs, and production engineering support. DFMA emerged as a key component of Lean operations several years after Lean Enterprise concepts were introduced. While there may have been scattered attempts made by companies to introduce DFMA in an attempt to standardize parts and reduce costs, DFMA grew in popularity with the implementation of Lean. However, many educators still do not include it today. In our experience, most production process Kaizen events have one or more recommendations relating to the ease of assembly improvements that could be achieved if there were design changes.

In our Lean Facilitator training course, we have expanded on the DFMA theory and encourage companies to take the concept even further. We recommend the concepts of DFMA for product design, process design (both manufacturing and administration), product line design, and ease of after sale service. This is a good application of the Value concept. Value for traditional design operations was geared more toward getting the product released to manufacturing and out into the marketplace. Lean has forced an enterprise view of the value stream and encourages cross-functional involvement early in the design phase to consider administration, assembly, user friendliness, and after-sale service.

DFMA also addresses the prevention of waste by not over-designing products, and by not adding costs for capability that exceeds the customer needs or expectations.

Executives in all corporate disciplines have been amazed by the volume, and quality, of design recommendations that have emerged from Kaizen teams that were staffed by non-technical personnel. When the focus is on the process, as it is with Kaizen, non-technical people can generate some great ideas that ultimately change the design of products. Design for ease of use (see below) can be applied to non-manufacturing products as well. Consider the design of software systems that administer businesses. These processes should not be over-designed. Simplicity will help to prevent the speed of the process from operating at a glacial pace.

DFMA and ease of use should be required considerations for every Kaizen event. While there may be some initial conflict with Design Engineering, eventually the concept of cross-functional participation in design activity will become the standard, and both the organization and the customer will benefit.

If your company processes a large amount of engineering changes once a product has been released to manufacturing, this is a good indication that you need to develop the DFMA concept.

DFEU

In most organizations, there is no formal process in place for designing procedures or office processes. As you review existing processes, you will find that most have evolved over time, and many have built-in reviews, approvals, or additional steps that resulted from an error that occurred longer ago than most people can remember.

As we review existing processes for value-added, non value-added and non value-added required steps, we are essentially reworking processes that should have been designed to prevent the waste in the first place.

What is Design for Ease of Use?

It is a conscious process of making design decisions only after fully evaluating the procedures, processes, tools, quality control measures and any equipment impacts. In order to optimize workflow in the office, the DFEU team must begin with some steps as follows:

- Process flows should be identified and documented.

- The VA, NVA and NVAR components of each flow must be identified, including identification of the customers (internal and external) for whom the value is provided.

- A cost/value ratio should be developed, if possible, to help determine what should be automated, what should be streamlined, and which steps should be eliminated or combined with others.

As you review administrative processes, ask and answer the following questions.

- How many steps are in the process?

- Is value added at each step?

- Does each activity in each step add value?

- How many wasteful activities will take place at each step such as waiting, filing, copying, etc.?

- How long should each step take?

- Why is the step necessary? What would happen if the step was eliminated?

- How many stops does the information make?

- How long is each stop?

- How long is each stop compared to the value added time for the activities within the step?

- What can go wrong at each step? Is it possible to make a mistake?

- If a mistake can be made, what can be done to prevent the mistake?

- If the mistake cannot be prevented, can it be detected prior to moving to the next stage?

- Would customers be willing to pay for this step if they knew about it?

Reinforce DFEU by creating Standard Work to ensure that each new process is repeatable and that it prevents variations. To avoid variations in the new process, investigate and consider the habits of the people and the organization that created the original wasteful process. Lean is about change and cannot be accomplished in a vacuum. A new process requires people and organizations that accept and can adapt to change.

Do everything possible to simplify the process or procedure. Simplification is a cornerstone of Lean. However, remember: simple is not easy!

Visual Workplace

The Visual Workplace is collection of memos, charts, graphs, schedules, Kanbans, Andons (lights or other electronic signals that indicate the status of a process or machinery), lines, and a wide variety of other indicators displayed throughout the workplace. Many of these will present the current status of operations compared with historical data and geared toward strategic and tactical Lean goals. Each work area in your plant should have a Visual Workplace display that reflects the status of operations, and equipment, including productivity, training, TPM, problem recognition and programs or plans to solve those problems.

When you tour a plant that has implemented a good Visual Workplace, you can do so and not have to ask a lot of questions. You will understand what each cell is producing, what rate it needs to produce at to meet customer demand, and what types of problems the cell has incurred recently. You will also be able to determine how the plant is performing to tactical and strategic goals.

A good rule to follow is to be generous with information. After employees have received a Lean education, they understand the significance of metrics such as inventory turns and material handling costs, and can relate their participation in the Lean transformation to the improvements that are being achieved.

A great visual technique is to display before and after pictures throughout the plant, so that anyone visiting the plant can see the improvements that you have made. The comparison of a wide angle picture of an old production line to that of a compact u-shaped production cell can be impressive.

The three light system mentioned earlier is a good example of Visual Workplace as well. The Visual Workplace fits perfectly with other programs that may also be in place. For example, a visual indication of the status of inventory complies with ISO regulations. Standard work can be a part of your visual workplace. Pictures showing assembly techniques and samples of products that have been assembled correctly are a great way to introduce and sustain a standard work initiative.

All information included in your Visual Workplace must be kept current. When we visit facilities that have performance metrics displayed it is very discouraging when we see that the information is out of date. There is an unlimited number of ways to visualize information and some of these are very creative. However, visual clutter should be avoided at all costs as this only confuses people. Make the information relevant and useful.

Takt Time

Takt Time is the time available to produce one unit, or the pace at which the production line needs to operate in order to meet the customer demand for product. Takt Time is calculated by dividing the total seconds available for manufacturing for a period of time by the total customer demand for that same time period.

When calculating the total seconds available for manufacturing you take the standard work day and deduct the time for scheduled breaks and other non-manufacturing events such as meetings. Takt Time will be reported in seconds, and it represents the number of seconds a production line has to manufacture and pack one item of product. If your process is operating faster than Takt Time you should slow the process down or stop it completely. If you are behind Takt Time you can work overtime to accommodate a spike in demand, or plan an additional shift if the demand is anticipated to be long-lived. You can also create an additional production cell to manufacture at a faster pace.

An Example

Acme Ltd. operates one 8 hour shift to manufacture Thermostats. The production workers get one-half hour for lunch and two ten minute breaks. Each production cell will have a ten minute meeting each morning, and ten minutes at the end of each day to clean their work areas.

The time available is 8hrs – 1hr and 10 min for non-production activity = 6hrs 50 minutes production time. This is 410 minutes or 24,600 seconds available for production.

For customer demand, use an ordering rate of 300 per day.

To calculate Takt Time, divide 24,600 by 300 = 82 seconds, meaning that Acme needs to manufacture one finished product every 82 seconds to meet demand. The time periods used for calculating time available for production and customer demand must be the same.

Lean follows the basic principle that you cannot manufacture any faster than the slowest process. When you are timing each production step, you will find the one process step that takes the longest time to perform.

If you divide that time into the time available, you will have a good indication of the maximum rate of production for the production cell. Once you know the maximum rate of production, you will know if you need to speed the process up or slow it down. Using the above Takt Time calculation, if your slowest process was 35 seconds you could produce products much faster than demand. If your slowest process took 90 seconds you would not be able to meet demand with the process as it currently exists.

The Five Whys

The 5 Whys is a simple method used to get to the root cause of problems or to determine why certain processes are done a certain way. For problems, the theory is that the first reason given for why something didn't work is rarely the root cause for failure. Regarding processes and the methods used to execute the process steps, the 5 Why Method can be used to reveal activities that have no real value.

This tool is also very useful during Kaizen events where the majority of the team is not familiar with the process being examined. Every step in the process should be challenged, and the 5 Why Method is a great way to do this. Soon, everyone will use this tool to validate the work that they, and others, are doing. Additionally, it does not take long for the people being asked about an error, or a process, to realize that you are going to be relentless in your pursuit of the root cause, or reason for the process step. When this happens, they will think twice before they give you an answer. Often times, accepting the first answer as the reason for an error or a process step can lead to embarrassment.

Example

Q. Why did the machine fail?

A. The motor burnt out.

Q. Why did the motor burn out?

A. The shaft seized.

Q. Why did the shaft seize?

A. There was no lubrication.

Q. Why was there no lubrication?

A. The filter was clogged.

Q. Why was the filter clogged?

A. It was the wrong size mesh.

One-Piece-Flow

One of the more difficult aspects of Lean can be convincing people that assembling one piece at a time is faster, and more efficient, than producing in batches.

Over the past few years, we have had to prove the effectiveness of one-piece-flow by actually demonstrating the concept to the non-believers. In a water meter plant in Germany, a supervisor challenged one-piece flow when the theory was presented in a Lean training class. We visited his production area after the training session and observed what the supervisor thought was a very effective way to assemble water meters. There were eight separate parts required to assemble a particular meter. After the water meter was assembled, it would move on to a test station that could test twelve water meters simultaneously. The assembly was performed by two individuals each having four process steps. The test area was loaded with trays of assembled water meters waiting to be tested.

The first point made to the supervisor was that the abundance of trays awaiting testing was an indication that assembly took much less time than testing, and there was a chance that one person could assemble twelve water meters and then pass them on to the test station, thereby eliminating one person in the assembly operation. The second point was that if there was anything wrong with the process, or the material used to assemble the large quantity of meters awaiting test, it would be very costly to rework the assembled meters. If the assembly operation was working at a pace that matched the testing process there should never be more than twelve or twenty four meters that were defective if an error was found. The tray of twelve meters was created for an obvious reason. If the water meter testing machine could test twelve meters, then the assembly operation should provide batches of twelve meters to the test station. The assembly technique was very simple; grab twelve pieces of the first part needed and place them in the correct location within the water meter base. This process would be repeated three times by the first operator. Then, the tray would be set aside for delivery to the next operator who would follow a similar process to add the last four parts.

As we observed these operators, we noticed that they would never grab the exact amount of parts, and would have to reach for additional parts or put excess parts back in the storage containers. On occasion, parts would fall onto the workbench or production floor. As they worked their way through the tray, the movement needed to place parts on meter bases increased.

After observing this process for approximately thirty minutes, we suggested that we experiment with a one person assembly process. We organized the water meter base and the seven additional parts in an area that could be reached easily, and began to assemble one water meter at a time. When we timed the new process, our original observation regarding the speed of assembly was confirmed. It would take many days of gathering quality statistics to prove that the new assembly technique was more cost effective than the original batch process. The supervisor became a Convert. On our next visit to the plant a month later, every water meter assembly operation had been converted to one-piece-flow. There was also a significant drop in the number of water meters that failed to pass the test.

This was a very simple challenge to the one-piece-flow theory. Not all operations are so easily transformed into one-piece-flow processes. The size of parts and the equipment used to assemble parts can have a significant impact on establishing one-piece-flow. If you keep one-piece-flow as your goal, you will be able to find ways to get there. It can take several iterations before you reach a layout, or process, that works in the most efficient manner. In a lot of cases, the workers who perform the processes will find creative ways to improve the flow after you have done the original work. If you have to design new processes, or equipment, to accommodate one-piece-flow, do it! The payback should be reached very quickly.

Line Balancing Chart

A line balancing chart depicts each process in a production line and the amount of time, expressed in seconds, that each process takes. Using the Line Balance Chart, you compare the longest production process time with the Takt Time to see if the line can meet the current customer demand. The chart will also indicate where processes can be combined, and still be performed as fast as the slowest process. This allows you to take people out of the process while continuing to meet demand.

A line balancing chart is one of the first activities that should be completed in a Kaizen event that is examining a production or administration process. This chart will provide the team with important information. Once the production process steps have been identified, they should be timed. The team should time each step ten times. Then deduct the best

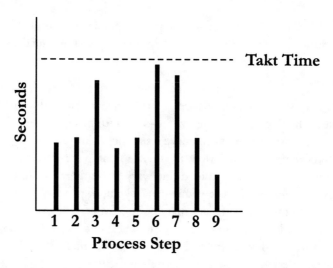

Figure 1.1 - As this sample Line Balancing Chart shows, process steps 1&2, 4&5, and 8&9 could be combined if the processes were close to each other; as a result, three people could be taken from this process. Additionally, with the balanced cell, there would be very little work-in-process inventory (six pieces).

and the worst times, and calculate an average process time using the eight remaining timings. Using an electronic spreadsheet, the calculations can be done quickly, and a line balancing chart can be incorporated into the spreadsheet design so that as the timings are completed the chart is created. The Takt Time for the product manufactured in the production line should be shown on the line balancing chart so that the team can compare the production process time to customer demand.

Curtain operations, those operations that take much longer than any other process step, will be obvious on the line balancing chart. If a curtain operation exists, and the chart shows that the production line can meet customer demand, there is a chance that process steps can be combined, and demand can still be met, as long as the combined process times do not exceed the Takt Time. If the curtain operation takes longer than Takt Time, there are some options that the team can pursue. They can investigate ways to improve the speed of the curtain operation. The team could consider duplicating the machinery, or adding an operator, to cut the operation time in half. Adding additional production shifts, or duplicating the entire process on a single shift is an option; however, this is a more costly solution and should be used only after all other options have been exhausted.

The line balancing chart can eliminate a lot of unnecessary conversation at the Kaizen presentation. The chart offers visual support for the team recommendations to improve the process. It is our experience that few senior production executives have ever seen such visual presentations of their production processes and take to the concept very quickly.

Spaghetti Charts

Spaghetti Charts depict material and people movement in a production process. Once the chart is complete, the total distance material and people travel to build a product or assembly is available. This chart is a valuable tool for Kaizen team members so that they can adequately represent the waste in the old process and reflect the efficiency created by the new process.

The charts are called "Spaghetti Charts" because they look like spaghetti when they are complete.

The chart is prepared by drawing a plant layout. The chart should be scaled so that distance calculations can be made accurately. Preparing these charts can be complicated and the accuracy must be confirmed and agreed to by the team. An index showing the parts and processes should be included on the chart and a separate color should be used for each part or assembly. It is not necessary to draw crooked lines to depict the lefts and rights that are made to get from one point in the plant to another. You can simply draw a straight line from the warehouse to a machine or assembly area; the scaled distance calculation is the important item.

It is not uncommon for these charts to indicate that material travels thousands of feet, if not a few miles, from the point where it first enters the building to the point from which it is shipped to an end customer. People movement would include the total distance traveled by material handlers, operators/assemblers, and changeover personnel.

The Kaizen team should be very precise when they prepare the Spaghetti Chart. Charts for the old, and the newly-created process, must be prepared. Usually, the presentation of these charts at the summary meeting is visually powerful. We often see that material and people movement is reduced by 90+% when Lean concepts are implemented. At one plant where several Lean production cells had already been created, we copied the original process Spaghetti Charts onto overhead slides and overlaid all of those charts onto an overhead projector; there were so many lines on these charts that the plant disappeared.

The rules of Lean that pertain to limiting people and material travel are reinforced when you prepare Spaghetti Charts. Few in your organization will contest the logic behind those rules when they view Spaghetti Charts that show product moving multiple times from the warehouse to the production floor, back to the warehouse, and back to the production floor.

U-Shaped Production Cells

It has been proven that a U-shaped cell, moving product clockwise through the process, and employing standard work, is the most efficient way to manufacture. People and machinery are placed close together allowing material to be handed to the next process, one piece at a time. While the Japanese say that the clockwise movement is best, we have seen a plant in Brazil that reversed this direction of flow and the cells work just fine.

In a typical straight-line production process there is less opportunity to balance production. It is not possible to combine those process steps that could be combined because of the distance and the sequential aspects of the process. The Line Balancing Chart is a good tool to use to explain this. As the chart shows, certain process steps can be combined because their combined process time is less than other single process steps. The problem is the requirement for sequential operations: step 3 must be done before step 6. In a typical production line, the distance between steps 3 and 6 could be

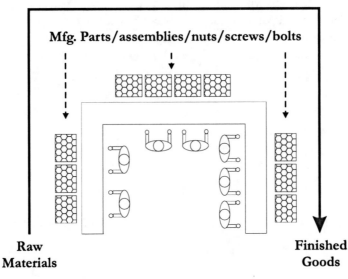

Figure 1.2 - A U-shaped production cell.

111

considerable. In a U-shaped cell, it could be possible for the assembler doing step 3 to pass an item across a table to an assembler who will perform step 4, and maybe step 5. That assembler then passes the part back to the assembler who originally performed step 3 so that he or she can perform step 6.

There could be any number of reasons why organizing a U-shaped cell could be difficult. The most common is the electrical connections. If the electrical connections, or controls, are located on the sides of machines it can cause a problem when you try to move the machines in a cell close together. Do not let this stop you; the advantages gained from moving machines closer together is worth the cost you will incur by moving the electrical or control boxes.

Another issue that you may have to address is the location of materials. If the parts used to assemble a specific product are small, there is usually no problem in organizing a U-shaped cell. The problem arises when there are bulky parts or assemblies needed to produce the product. Be creative and you will come up with a solution to the space problem. We have seen cells where plastic plumbing tubes were used to deliver small parts to cramped spaces by loading overhead buckets with parts, and letting the laws of gravity work to deliver parts to an assembler working below.

Rabbit Chase

Rabbit Chase is a production technique that has individual production workers walking through a U-shaped cell performing each step necessary to produce a finished product. Using this technique, a plant can vary the rate of production to meet non-linear customer demand.

We used the Rabbit Chase method in a plant in Mexico to produce a product that experienced wide ranges in demand over periods of time. The Rabbit Chase operation was able to keep up with high demand as well as contend with periods where the demand was well below the production capability of the cell. Also, applying this technique in Mexico, where attendance can be sporadic, keeps the production cell producing at least at some level.

The Rabbit Chase technique is also ideal for creating a cell where all of the operators are cross-trained. You will get some variation on the rate of production using a Rabbit Chase. Not all workers will be equally proficient at each operating step. Because of this, you should use the average time of three or four workers to perform a production step when balancing a Rabbit Chase cell. Doing this will help you meet a certain predictable rate of manufacturing.

Focused Factory

A focused factory is a plant layout that has production cells that include all of the equipment, and personnel, needed to make a particular product, or series of products. A modified version of the Focused Factory can be established in cases where one, or more, machines are used to satisfy parts or assemblies for multiple products. Metal stamping and painting are good examples of machines or processes that might be used on different products throughout your plant.

If your plant manufactures a wide range of products, it is a good idea to establish a focused factory for each major product group. The speed of your implementation could be improved by taking the focused factory approach. Each focused factory will be able to implement change at its own pace and the program will not come to a standstill if a difficult problem should arise in any one area.

One company where we assisted in the implementation of Lean made the decision to establish four separate factories. As management allocated machines to the individual factories, the machines were cleaned and moved to their respective focused factory locations. After each machine was cleaned and moved, it was painted a specific color to match the color chosen for that factory. You knew which factory you were in because of the color of the machines. They also color-coded pallets and containers so that material handlers could simply deliver material to the front of each process based on the color of the container. This eliminated the paper that was needed to control material flow in the old system.

The focused factory can also facilitate your move to point-of-use inventory storage and eliminate the main warehouse.

2

The Need for Change

If you change the way you look at things,
the things you look at will change.
- Unknown

As we mentioned early in this book, there is a panic in U.S. industry today. While this is due to global competition, the root cause of the problem is that the processes used to conduct business are wasteful, out of control, and very costly.

To better understand the situation we are in today, we need to discuss the two primary aspects of the typical manufacturing business separately.

Manufacturing

Most non-Lean companies are employing some form of batch-and-queue manufacturing. Various departments spread throughout the manufacturing facilities are fabricating parts, or assemblies, and these eventually wind up in a final assembly department where the finished products are produced.

There are many problems with this method of production. First of all, the production is usually scheduled using some form of Materials Requirements Planning (MRP) as the base. MRP-based production schedules are a combination of actual customer orders and forecasted demand that aim for maximum productivity from both people and machines. The result of this is that most companies build and warehouse huge inventories, while historically, annual inventory turns of U.S. manufacturing organizations (non-automotive) has only been somewhere between four and six.

Problems and Waste Related to Manufacturing

Material Handling - It is not unusual to have raw material moved from the warehouse to a sub-assembly department and then back to the warehouse. Sub-assemblies are then picked from the warehouse and delivered to a final assembly operation, and go back to the warehouse again. Pick lists representing customer orders are then issued to the warehouse for ultimate customer delivery. Materials can be moved many times, and travel thousands of feet through the process, requiring material handlers and a fleet of forklift or other material conveyance equipment. Each movement is supported by an administrative process which requires the creation and control of paper or electronic data. Sudden changes in the production schedule, due to changing customer priorities, can add additional material handling.

Financial Control - With such large inventories on-hand there is a need for verification and control. Cycle counting and periodic physical inventories are the standard mechanisms to accomplish this.

Obsolescence/Scrap – Ordering material and producing goods prior to an actual demand can cause problems. Engineering changes can obsolete raw material if not administered properly, and poor workmanship often leads to scrap.

Rework - Engineering changes can also require rework of subassemblies, and finished goods, that have been produced in advance of actual demand. Poor workmanship typically results in rework and sometimes scrap.

Lost/Damaged Goods – Raw material, parts, sub-assemblies and finished goods can be lost, stolen, or damaged if they are produced in advance of actual customer demand.

Scheduling – Scheduling production when forecasts, and customer demands, change in the short term can be troublesome. There can be several iterations of the daily, weekly or monthly production plans.

Expediting – When actual demand varies from the forecasted demand or when suppliers fail to perform, there is a significant amount of expediting that often takes place. Supplier order cancellation fees and expedited freight costs can eat away at profits.

Overtime – Actual demand is the usual cause of overtime in a production facility. Production time taken to produce forecasted demand requires overtime work to produce actual demand within the same time period. This frequently happens when companies make promises to key customers regarding on time delivery.

Productivity – Historically, management has sought to maximize the use of people and machines. Full utilization of people time has driven the need to have machines operating continuously. Preventive maintenance is rarely performed resulting in premature and frequent machine downtime. With the maximization of people and machines, many plants have become dirty and, in some cases, dangerous.

Poor Quality – Few companies focus on design and assembly to ensure the best quality. Most have costly quality control systems that accommodate the lack of good design and assembly processes. Many companies have established mediocre quality guidelines that also accommodate, rather than fix, process, or material related problems.

Management – Management is inclined to maintain the status quo. They spend their time working around known process problems and cannot seem to get together to solve the cross-functional issues. There is likely to be reasonable cooperation between managers within the major disciplines, but the turf issues that arise from functional silos can be detrimental to a business if the management team is allowed to operate in an autonomous fashion.

People – A tremendous resource is being wasted. Historically, change programs have been driven by management and the active participation by factory or clerical workers in these change programs has been rare.

Administration

The administration aspects of business have become very complex. The reasons for this are two-fold. First, and more difficult to change, are the third party requirements forced upon business because of the legal and tax authorities. You have no choice but to conform to the various legal statutes that control business operations, and to the local, state, and federal tax regulations. Public companies have additional obligations for reporting, and conforming to, the rules and regulations of the Securities and Exchange Commission. Companies with significant debt are usually required to do additional reporting, and are subject to lending provisions that can cause additional administrative overhead. This is not to say that you cannot develop more efficient ways to conform to these requirements.

Secondly, are the inefficient processes that have developed as a result of micro-management or the lack of vision to develop processes that are capable (error-proofed) of providing value solely to the end customers. Side issues with regard to management that both authors have encountered are the scope of control, and size of an organization. These are ego metrics that have added to the chaos and cost of business. If you have experienced the latter, you know what we are talking about. If you are not aware of this phenomenon, then you are fortunate, and will have less to fix in your organization.

Problems/Waste Relating to Administration

While there is a vast amount of waste in most administrative processes we will focus on two that have been present in every administrative Kaizen event that we have been associated with.

Reporting – Administrative personnel spend huge amounts of time gathering, organizing, and reporting data that is historical and of questionable relevance. The number of people involved in this activity is usually much greater than the number of individuals who receive the results. Software manufacturers have created user-friendly means to organize, and report, data that are under-utilized by most companies. Much of the clerical activity could be eliminated if certain individuals in the organization would learn how to retrieve this data themselves. When you become active in administrative Kaizen events, be sure to include a review of every report used by every department to ensure that those reports are relevant.

Approvals – Managers, who wish to impose their authority on the organization, by approving every last detail, add a substantial amount of time and cost to the business process. We would estimate that ninety plus percent of the time taken to complete the administration of business is wasted. When you master the value stream mapping concept of Lean, this statistic will not surprise you. Keith once reviewed the requisition and other documentation required for a job that he ultimately accepted at a Fortune 500 company. There were at least 10 signatures on the requisition, and half that number on the document that created the offer letter. Keith was also surprised to hear that he was selected as the ultimate candidate for the job early in the process that took over 5 weeks to conclude.

Another anecdote relating to approvals, that is even more disturbing, is that of an executive in a Fortune 500 company who was given a long term jail sentence, because he had signed an expense report that included a payoff to the purchasing executive in a major U.S. city for agreeing to purchase product from that executive's company. The argument given by the defense in this case was that no executive has the time to review everything that they are required to approve and that the executive in question had no operational authority over the individual who made the payment.

Why Change?

If any of the above situations are applicable to your company you have a need to change. It is rare however, that we hear of a company that wants to become Lean because they have recognized that their processes are broken. Often the primary reason for wanting to become a Lean organization is the current impact on the business from low cost producing countries.

At a supplier Lean Mastery course that we conducted for one of our clients, we had over twenty companies represented that ranged in size from fifteen employees to several thousand employees. Every one of these companies reported that they were losing business to competitors in Asia. Another interesting fact is that every student in this supplier training course was from a manufacturing discipline. Every company that sent students to our class believed that the solution to their problems resided somewhere in the manufacturing operation. The bad news was that only one company sent a senior executive for training. Unfortunately, this scenario has become a trend in all of the training courses that we have conducted, either at company locations, or at the universities where we teach Lean. The primary response to global competition in the U.S. seems to be downsizing or moving operations overseas.

Downsizing often produces internal chaos. In our opinion, many executives saddled with the responsibility for downsizing have lost touch with the internal workings of their companies, and do not have accurate process, and financial data, to properly plan and execute a successful downsizing plan.

Lean is a rightsizing plan. The difference between a Lean plan and a typical downsizing plan is that the Lean plan focuses on value, and the processes used to deliver that value to the downstream customer. An effective Lean plan will eliminate a substantial amount of the operating costs incurred by the typical mass manufacturing operation. Poorly planned and executed downsizing programs will likely create a financial and human resource nightmare. The surviving employees are expected to assume the responsibilities of their recently terminated colleagues, and have little conviction that the executives in the company have a clue about how the company actually works. The likely response of employees to a downsizing program is that they will attempt to find another job. Unfortunately the best employees are the ones likely to find new jobs, and leave early, adding to the chaos. Service, quality, and productivity starts to decline which adds additional costs and customers continue to leave.

A recent example is the mortgage arm of a regional bank that reduced its workforce by 15%. The employees who were laid off were asked to leave the same day they received notification. The remaining employees had no prior knowledge of the impending downsizing and no attempt was made to change the processes, so that they could be operated effectively. Six weeks later, there was chaos. Customers were complaining that the services were too slow, or that major errors were being made. The bank then went out and hired temporaries to help solve the problem. Some of these temporaries were people they had recently laid off.

In our opinion, downsizing is a poor strategy employed by management that does not recognize that it is the business processes that are inadequate, not the people. We have been with companies that have attempted downsizing programs. In many cases, the ultimate cost of the downsizing program exceeded expectations and the end result was even more devastating than the initial threat to the business.

Moving operations offshore can be as devastating as a downsizing program if it is poorly conceived and poorly executed. Our Lean Math chapter will cover this offshore operations strategy and provide insight into the costs that are incurred, but are rarely considered, during the critical planning phase.

There is no question that the competitive threat will remain and even grow. We practically ensure that by transferring our technology to these overseas locations. Businesses that have failed to control their processes and costs, coupled with government's attempts to manage global economics have contributed to the manufacturing wastelands that are now appearing all over our country. The key question is how to combat the threat. One thing is certain; business as usual will not be an effective response.

With the advent of the Internet, companies are able to shop around and find suppliers that, in previous times, would have been unknown to them. Today, companies can, and do, make decisions about your business just by looking at your website. You may never get the opportunity to discuss your capabilities or quote on a particular job. Business to Business (B2B) auctions allow companies to find new, and low cost, suppliers that they would never have located in the past. Being a Lean supplier will not guarantee you a share of this type of business. However, if you are not Lean, you will almost certainly be excluded from it. The available pool of low cost labor continues to grow. Global politics has an effect on global markets. Tariffs on imports are a perfect example of global politics in action; The "Most Favored Nation" status is another. Industries like textiles, shoes, and steel have slowly disappeared from the domestic scene. For those of us old enough to remember, the first move in this migration of U.S. industries was made by companies that moved to the south to avoid the high cost of labor in the north. Southern state and municipal governments created tax incentives and legislated "right to work laws" as a lure to attract companies in the north who were experiencing high operating costs as well as labor union issues.

A colleague once suggested, with tongue in cheek, that our company should just acquire an old aircraft carrier and populate it with all of our manufacturing equipment. We could then just sail to the country with the cheapest labor and move on when that labor becomes too expensive. In effect, that is what is happening today - without the aircraft carrier of course.

Competing effectively will require a radical change in the way we operate our businesses.

Before we go further, we should say that Lean Enterprise concepts are effective regardless of the industry in which you operate. We frequently hear that "Lean is fine for other businesses but not for ours." This is not true. Every business is made of a series of processes that produce a product or provide a service. Lean focuses on those processes to eliminate the waste that is inherent in processes that were developed from a "mass manufacturing" or "control at all cost" mentality.

The need to change should be driven by a desire to establish processes that deliver value; processes that do exactly what they were intended to do. The organizations that exist today are a reflection of the management that created them.

These management teams were merely a collection of executives whose primary vision was the success of their respective organizations, and perhaps their personal survival. How else could you explain the position that many companies find themselves in today? Overhead costs are through the roof; short term financial results cannot be predicted with any degree of accuracy; operating within prescribed scrap, rework, and production yield benchmarks are considered to be valid performance metrics; any endeavor requiring cross-functional cooperation is a nightmarish journey that never seems to have an end; loyal customers and loyal employees are terms that are now considered oxymoron's; value and the processes used to deliver that value are decades old and do not meet customer expectations; and on and on.

Management is in a perpetual problem containment mode. Substituting the pain and expense of the containment mode with that of a change mode is the vision that needs to materialize and prevail. The primary goal of a business executive should be the profitable perpetuation of the business. In our opinion, the first step in reaching this goal is an admission that the current processes are broken. The second step would be to commit to change.

Changing Management Thinking

While there are a number of visionary mangers out there, they are certainly in the minority. We are talking about the lack of demonstrated capability of management, in general, to harness, lead and inspire continuous improvement activity as a way of life in business.

During one of our Lean courses, one student completed a required Kaizen project that would have resulted in a cost reduction of $120,000 for his company. When the project was presented to his management, he was told to slow down, and take a more conservative approach. There was no risk associated with the project, and it could have been completed in a week. It was obvious that the 'not invented here' (NIH) syndrome was in play. That project has never been implemented, and the employee has now moved on to another company where his talent and creativity is encouraged. Since his departure, his former company has been downsizing and struggling to stay competitive. To this day, we cannot understand why he was sent on the course in the first place.

We have found that most employees are eager to participate in activity that will improve the financial performance, and competitiveness, of the business. They look at this as a contribution to their own job security, and it allows them to be involved in a meaningful way. Management, on the other hand, has a tendency to see this as a threat to their power, or status, and they are often uncomfortable with this change. Directly or indirectly, they block improvements through their actions or words. In one company that was going Lean the plant manager was present for Kaizen project presentations one Friday morning. Hearing something he did not agree with he blurted out "that is the most stupid thing I have ever heard" (His words, not ours). The list of volunteers for future Kaizen dwindled as a result of this behavior.

We have seen countless examples of management ineptitude when it comes to leading Lean initiatives. They are, by far, the single biggest category of concrete heads. In one plant, the production managers ruled with an iron fist, and employees were not inclined to make suggestions that might improve the process. These managers were, and continue to ignore the mandate for the institutionalization of Lean in the hope that the company is not committed to the program. Today, this plant is struggling to provide product to customers on time, and profitability levels are not where they could be.

Some years ago, before the advent of Lean, when Brian was running a manufacturing plant, he initiated a weekly forum to allow employees to express their views, offer suggestions, or just simply attend to keep informed. It took a long time before employees believed that they could say what was on their minds without fear of retribution. One employee eventually made a suggestion that would result in a significant improvement. When asked why he had not raised this before, he said "the last time I made a suggestion was 20 years ago, and at that time I was told that if I didn't like it here they were hiring across the street". Lack of respect, indifference, verbal abuse and a host of other demeaning offenses will stay with employees for a very long time.

In contrast, another of our clients judges its managers by their ability to relate to employees, and to get them involved in continuous improvement activity. When you enter that company, you 'feel the difference'. The attitude is so positive and so similar throughout the entire workforce that you begin to suspect that they are cloning them. This company was very successful even before Lean, and they are using Lean to enhance their financial performance and competitive position further. They have also declared that there will be no job losses due to implementing Lean.

127

Effective managers will coach and facilitate. They are self-assured, and understand that the success of their employees will reflect positively on them. We are fond of saying that recognition defies the laws of gravity. It invariably flows uphill. Good managers understand that, and great managers make improvements happen. In companies that are not well managed, you will find employees aspiring to mediocrity.

A Good Offense is the Best Defense

Many companies respond to competitive threats in a defensive mode. Price cutting, consignment inventories, or other margin-reducing actions are offered to retain customers. On a recent travel assignment, Keith encountered an executive of a company that supplies parts to a division of one of the biggest U.S. corporations. This man had just received a letter from his customer that outlined part costs each year for the next five years; and they were not going up.

Every price cutting exercise is a reduction in margin unless it is offset by a cost reduction. One client recently told us that he was about to say goodbye to a customer he had been supplying for about 25 years. He simply could not afford to cut the price of his product any further. Until he was introduced to Lean, he could see no other alternative than to cut the cord.

Has any of the following occurred recently in your company?

- You have lost an order to a competitor on price.

- You are having increasing difficulty maintaining margin due to price erosion, or rising manufacturing costs.

- One of your competitors has introduced a version of a new product that you were developing, and you are still months away from introduction.

- You are being forced by your customers to consign inventory, or maintain guaranteed levels of finished goods, because there is a lack of confidence in your ability to deliver on time.

- You are working overtime, or building inventory, because customers are demanding that you match the shorter lead times that are being offered by your competitors.

- You are losing business because your products contain features that the customer is unwilling to pay for.

- One of your distant competitors has become one of your main competitors.

If any of these issues is familiar to you, do you know the reason? Is your competitor a Lean enterprise? If the answer is yes, how will you react? If the answer is no, how long will it be before the competitor is Lean?

Visionary leaders are using Lean Enterprise as a strategic weapon to increase the distance between their companies and the competition. Lean Enterprise will not go away. Companies that are not Lean will suffer a distinct competitive disadvantage, or even go out of business. Lean Enterprise is powerful and it will be extremely difficult to bridge the competitive gap unless you are at least operating on a level playing field.

Implementing Lean enterprise is an offensive change strategy that will help to position your business with the best possible cost structure. Additionally, you will likely see significant improvements in product quality and service levels. Inventories will be reduced drastically, and you will make better use of your existing assets. Products will get to market faster and will be designed using concepts that make them easy to manufacture, at the best cost. Cash flow will improve, and you will experience levels of participation, and creativity, from employees you may never have thought possible. Lean is not some new brand of snake oil; it is a process that addresses many of the strategic, and tactical, needs of your business. Regrettably, it will have limited benefit unless you can execute it properly.

2 - The Need for Change

Our experience with companies that are making the Lean transition is that they are experiencing significant shifts in operating results.

- Productivity improvements between 25% to 40%.

- Manufacturing space reductions up to 50%

- Inventory levels reduced to a few days supply, instead of a few months supply.

- 20% year on year improvements in cash generation through lower inventories, and lower investment.

- Virtual elimination of defects while improving product quality and reliability.

- Concurrent reduction in lead times and improvements in on-time shipments performance.

- Products designed that use simplified manufacturing techniques, and that have Six-Sigma quality levels designed in.

- Everyone in the organization involved in a continuous improvement activity permanently.

- Monthly accounting close reduced to a couple of days instead of a couple of weeks.

- Machines operating for months without unscheduled downtime.

- Set-up times dramatically reduced to produce smaller and more frequent lots.

- Facilities that are showcases that can be used as effective marketing tools.

Improvements like these (some are claiming even better results) are being achieved today by companies that are implementing Lean Enterprise. These are not aspirations; they are real accomplishments. This is the beef. If you are not implementing Lean, how will you compete with results like these?

If it has not already done so, the need for Lean will eventually arrive at your door. The key issue is whether you will implement Lean voluntarily, or whether you will be forced to implement it by a customer or a competitor. The Lean Enterprise concepts can be learned by anyone. Those who adopt and implement Lean concepts will have the distinct advantage.

Administrative Waste

A substantial amount of human resources and monies has been expended providing systems of administrative and financial control. Rather than create processes that were waste free and fool-proof, controls requiring review and approval were implemented that added costs and usually reduced the speed at which the process operated.

As an example, the cost of an R&D department in many companies can constitute up to 5% (or more) of sales. When a new product is released approximately 70% of the product cost is fixed. Later, when cost reductions are required, it is usually the manufacturing group that is tasked with the project. However, as you can see, there is little remaining discretionary cost left to work with.

Another example is the cost of inventory. Executives at the Toyota company are on record as having estimated inventory carrying costs to be as high as 30% of the cost of the inventory. This estimate is coming from a company that experiences very low rates to borrow money. The bulk of the high inventory carrying costs come from the cost of warehousing operations, handling, obsolescence, and control programs such as cycle counting and physical inventories.

It is much more difficult to pinpoint waste in the administrative areas than it is on the shop floor. Normally, manufacturing operations perform a clearly defined task and the output is readily apparent. In the office, employees perform multiple tasks across multiple departments, and it is significantly more difficult to judge the effectiveness of the output. Some companies measure and manage their indirect labor spending based on ratios of blue collar to white collar workers. Lean thinkers would not be comfortable with such a ratio; they will examine the value stream for delivering products and services, and eliminate the non-value added activity.

While certain administrative functions may appear necessary, many have little value-added benefit. Let us look at some examples.

- If you have a customer service department, why was it created in the first place? Was it because your processes, and resulting products, were unable to provide the necessary satisfaction levels and you needed a first line of defense?

- Why do all of your orders have to go through an order-entry function and on to a scheduling operation when it is likely that, on average, approximately 80% of all orders could go directly to the shop floor?

- Do you have a comprehensive budgeting process, and, at the same time, require the budget owner to go through an approval process when spending is needed?

- Do you have an army of accountants and administrators that gather historical data such as scrap, rework, production yields, production and productivity data? If you fix your process problems, the need to measure certain activities will not be necessary because the impact of such costs will be much less significant.

- Do you have a quality group? If so, why? Is it a policing operation because there is insufficient confidence in the integrity of the product, or service, being produced?

- How long does it take to make an engineering change? And, what is the cost in obsolescence for a product that was not designed properly or released prematurely?

There are many other examples and the entire administrative process needs to be evaluated and challenged. Is the customer paying you to perform these activities?

It can be said that the processes used to transact business and produce products in many companies are wasteful. The focus has not been on eliminating problems permanently. Every company has a few miracle workers who somehow manage to get things done amongst the chaos. These people are revered, and often times promoted, for their ability to get things done. When these miracle workers get into management positions, they prolong the chaos because their primary skill is working around the process.

A question that is often asked of job applicants is "how well do you work under stress?" If you are asked this question, you should have serious reservations about the operating mode in that company. While it would probably limit your opportunity to get the job, you should counter this question with a the question "what causes the stress in this company?" Let's continue the fantasy and say that the response to your question is any one of the following;

- Our management is constantly changing priorities.

- Our processes fail to provide accurate data.

- Any program requiring cross-functional cooperation is a nightmare.

- Your future boss is a tyrant.

- Our product price file is a conundrum.

- Our quality is at Three-Sigma.

- We can never meet a product release date.

- Our machinery is constantly breaking down, and we have no total productive maintenance program.

- Production is scheduled based on the loudest customer.

- We need to close the books early, so that we can have the time to massage the numbers to meet executive expectations.

- Our on-time delivery is 90%.

- Our sales forecasts are not reliable.

- We have never had an effective process improvement program at this company.

- Our advertised lead times are not attainable.

Many of these responses are more common than you might imagine. The focus in these companies is on finding people that can work around their broken processes and work in a chaotic environment.

In our experience, career progression and financial compensation has been based on working with mediocre processes that only contained problems and sustained non-value added activities. Take a look at your own personnel evaluation and bonus programs. Do these programs include words like maintain, sustain, continue etc., or do they contain words like change, create, or solve? If your company does not have an improvement program that is challenging every aspect of your business, there is a need for change.

The first major step in contemplating a Lean enterprise is to recognize the need for change. In the next chapter, we discuss the process of change and why there must be a compelling reason to do so, if the initiatives are to be successful. If the need for change, and where change is needed, is not clearly understood, Lean will be elusive.

The Process of Change

There is nothing more difficult to plan, more
doubtful of success, nor more dangerous to
manage than the creation of a new system.
For the initiator has the enmity of all who
would profit by the preservation of the old
system and the merely lukewarm defenders
in those who would gain by the new one.

- Machiavelli

It is amazing how many companies try to undertake a major
project, or culture transformation, and give little, or no,
consideration to the process of change. Change agents are
often tasked with the implementation, and have little understanding of the psychology of change.

The next time you hold a meeting, and everyone is sitting comfortably, ask them to get up and switch seats. Listen to the disgruntled comments, and you will get a small inkling of how the majority of people feel about change.

Psychologists will tell you that people do not naturally embrace change, even if it demonstrated to be for their own good. Change is perceived as an unwanted interruption to their daily routines. Most people will not willingly move out of their comfort zones. It generally takes at least six months for people to adjust to major changes, and sometimes significantly longer.

The Lean transformation is likely to involve major change for every function and person in the organization. In a typical Lean transformation, some 10-15% of people will become enthusiastic leaders. Some 70-80% will be non-committed, and even fearful of the change. These people can be brought on board provided they understand the purpose, and benefits, of the change. Finally, some 10-15% will be unwilling to change, and may even become concrete heads. Over time, you can win over some of these concrete heads, but limit your patience, and be firm in your conviction that achieving the best process is the only goal.

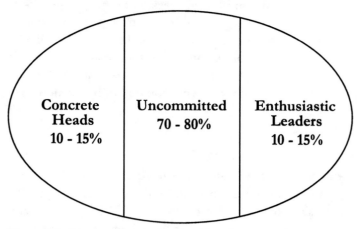

Figure 3.1 - Not everyone who is affected by a Lean transformation will support the initiative.

If you are managing this change, it is important to understand this profile, and to recognize that the change process needs to be managed, as well as the project itself.

There are many books available on the subject of change and it is worthwhile reading up on this subject. One of our favorites is *Leading Change* by John P. Kotter.[1]

It is important to understand the reasons why we often fail to get the results we expect, and what can be done to ensure success. Here are some of the reasons why change is not effective. In essence, we follow the framework outlined in Kotter's book but have adjusted it based on our own interpretations, observations and experience with Lean transformations.

---

[1] *Leading Change.* John P Kotter Harvard Business School Press 1996

Complacency

- For people to change there must be a compelling reason to do so. It is important that people understand why the change is necessary, and they need to be able to see how the change will benefit the organization, and ultimately themselves.

- Past successes may lead people to believe that the impending changes apply to someone else, and not to them, because they are doing their job just fine.

- Previous low performance expectations, or standards, can lead people to believe that the impending changes carry unrealistic expectations, and they will simply opt out.

- People may believe that, based on prior initiatives, they can 'ride it out' as things will inevitably return to their prior state, as they have done in the past.

No Coalition

- In any major change, a coalition (team) is needed to guide the process, and that coalition must grow significantly over time.

- Unless the organization is small, it is unlikely that any one individual, however charismatic, will have all of the assets needed to overcome inertia, or complacency. In fact, if there is no team or coalition, that individual is likely to burn out, or become disenchanted unless real progress is being made.

- Without a guiding and growing coalition, opposing forces will eventually undermine the change initiatives.

- This concept goes beyond executive commitment, which is a prerequisite to any change initiative. Management support is vital, but a coalition, with ever-increasing membership will help to ensure that this commitment becomes reality.

Lack of Vision

- If you want enthusiastic support for a change initiative, a sensible vision is needed. People must understand the true purpose of the change, and have an understanding of how life will be better once the change has been accomplished.

- After creating a compelling sense of urgency, and creating a guiding coalition there is little more important than communicating a sensible vision.

- A sensible vision helps to direct, align and inspire actions. However, the vision should be clear enough so that people can understand it in terms of how they can contribute. One of the key strategies of a Lean enterprise is Policy Deployment, and we will discuss this later in the book. Having a clear and sensible vision is fundamental to Policy Deployment success.

- Where there is no clear vision, the change effort becomes a confusing list of incompatible, time-consuming projects that have no direction. There is little sense of priority, and it is difficult to ensure that the available resource is applied to the efforts that are deemed most important to produce the desired outcome.

- In many failed transformations, you find the plans and programs themselves trying to play the role of the vision. This is risky, because when any given program has been completed there is often a sense that the 'vision' has been accomplished.

Poor planning

- In a Lean enterprise transformation, it is important to understand the transition phases. For example, in the early phases there is usually a significant amount of 'low-hanging fruit' to be picked. The process then settles down into a continuous improvement mode where more and more autonomy is passed on to employees. Over time, the progression is from a few large visible projects with potentially large returns to many improvement projects with smaller returns. The cumulative effect of the latter typically remains substantial, as long as the momentum is maintained.

- The strategic Lean plan can span a three to five year horizon. However, the tactical Lean planning horizon should be shorter (about 1 year). The plans should always be subject to review and adjustment. We see so many operations where the plan itself becomes the focus of attention as opposed to the improvement process. You can be certain that as soon as you begin implementation the plan will begin to change. To use a military term, 'no plan survives first contact'. Planning should be based on the best available information at the time, and then you should begin implementation, and adjust as you go.

- We often see a Lean implementation underway with no plan in place. We are astonished at the lack of direction, and milestones, but nonetheless there are expected financial outcomes included in the budgets or fiscal projections. We will discuss planning in more detail later in this book. It is very important that a Lean plan include certain key elements and we will cover these in some detail.

Poor Communication

- As mentioned earlier, major change is impossible unless most people are willing to help. Those same people must believe that the change is possible, or there will be little assistance given. It is critically important that sufficient time be devoted to communicating the compelling need to change, the vision, the role that individual employees can play, the progress being achieved, and the amount that remains to be accomplished.

- Without credible communication, hearts and minds will never be captured.

- It is also important to understand that communication is a two-way process. Feedback is required, and that feedback should be used to monitor and adjust. This will help employees develop a sense of ownership, and they will tackle future tasks more readily once they know their opinion is valued.

- Communication is a combination of both words and deeds with the latter being the most important. Too often, we see actions that totally contradict the words. Unless your message is credible, you are unlikely to get the support you need. It is vitally important that you 'walk the walk'.

Allowing obstacles to prevent progress

- Even when employees embrace change, they will be disempowered by huge obstacles in the way. For example, the traditional company is functionally organized, and activities that cross these functional boundaries are subject to varying levels of support. Unless the change is seen as having top priority, one or more of these functions is likely to prevent progress due to resource, or other, conflicts.

- Obstacles are sometimes mental, and sometimes physical. Sometimes they are people who are just simply unwilling to change. Well-placed blockers can halt an entire change effort, and management must ensure that this does not happen. It should be very clear that there will be zero tolerance for this type of action.

- Compensation and performance systems can be used very effectively to help people make the right choice between the new vision and self-interest.

Few short-term wins

- Real transformation takes time, and the risk of momentum loss can be offset by short-term wins. These wins need to be made visible to everyone.

- If no progress is visible, people are likely to join the resistance movement.

- We cannot just assume, or hope for, short-term wins. We must make them happen.

- It is important to sustain the sense of urgency over the long term. This can be achieved by publicizing gains, and through communication.

Declaring victory too soon

- Changing the culture of any organization takes a long time, and the new approaches are fragile, and subject to regression, especially in the early stages.

- Premature victory celebrations can stop all momentum so it is necessary to qualify all wins in terms of the plan status.

- It is important to celebrate wins, but this should not be an admission that the job is done.

- It is helpful to have someone available who will constantly challenge you to go to the next level. If you are not comfortable with this, you are unlikely to be comfortable with Lean.

Not anchoring changes in the culture

- Despite the fact that we are trying to 'change the way we do things around here', Lean will not be successful until it becomes 'the way we do things around here.'

- Until the new behaviors are rooted in the corporate culture, they are subject to regression, as soon as the pressure is removed.

- We need to show people how specific behaviors, and attitudes, have helped to improve performance.

- The changes should be associated with the implementation of the corporate vision, not the change agent, or some charismatic leader.

- All corporate activities, including succession, should reinforce the new behaviors. Too often, we see new management come on board, and dismiss all previous initiatives only to be replaced with their own. This permeates the flavor of the month concept.

There is no question that change is difficult. By focusing on the change process and the Lean process at the same time, we greatly increase the opportunity for success. As a rule of thumb, psychologists estimate that it takes between 6 and 18 months for someone to adjust to a major change in their life.[2] The changes initiated by Lean are major. If you are

---

[2] Adapted from the article "The Psychology of Change" by George P. Koenigsaecker

managing this change process, you should understand that employees, who are still in the 6-18 month transition period, are not going to be enthusiastic supporters of major change.

The faster you change, the faster you can improve productivity and performance. The overall organization will reject the change initiative if too many employees still pine for the old ways. As you push, encourage, and cajole, you should check to see if the guiding coalition is growing. This change characteristic, when combined with the learning curve, has another implication for change agents; in the first twelve months of the transformation process, you will have to drive it. Do not expect it to be driven from the bottom until you have established considerable momentum.

As people become believers in Lean, they are likely to become intolerant of waste. This may cause some difficulty working with people who have not yet come aboard. While there is a Lean conversion process for the organization as a whole, there is also a separate one for each individual.

At any given point in time, you will be persuading some people, and coaching others. Successful change will involve both authoritarian and participative management styles, simultaneously. This is not easy to do, and you need to be careful that you do not send mixed messages. Lean will not become a self-sustaining cultural change unless everyone is on board after three to five years of persistent effort. You must constantly assess where individuals are on their personal learning curve.

As they become confident with Lean concepts, you evolve to being their coach by stepping out of the way, except to help remove obstacles. Finally, a great way to think about change comes from an analogy by Fujio Cho, president of the Toyota Motor Company. He observed that organizations are like the human body. When a change is introduced, the body automatically creates antibodies that attack the change. When you try something new, expect the organization to attack it. In fact, the stronger the organization's culture, the more aggressively it will produce anti-bodies, and the more resistant it is to change.

Change in a Lean transformation should be accomplished through Kaizen. Kaizen is the power of Lean. Any attempt to accomplish the implementation of Lean concepts without Kaizen is a recipe for failure. Our experience shows that organizations which have failed to recognize the power of Kaizen are moving at a snails pace, and it is unlikely that they will ever reap the total benefit of Lean. Preventing the involvement of everyone will inhibit the creation of a Lean Culture.

When you focus on the process of change, in parallel with the Lean initiatives, Lean becomes less elusive.

Institutionalizing Lean

You have to inform to transform.
- Brian Furlong

A few years ago, we received a call from a potential client who had an interesting proposition. They had been implementing Lean for about three years, and had experienced some limited success. A new president (someone we have come to regard as a visionary leader) had just come on board, and he was not satisfied with the rate of progress. The proposition he put to us was to institutionalize Lean in his division.

Following an assessment and much discussion, we developed a process that we have since successfully applied at this and other client locations. The underlying problem was that, after three years, Lean was still considered a project that involved a relatively small percentage of the workforce. The president wanted Lean concepts understood, and applied daily by everyone in the company. In other words, Lean needed to be *'the way things are done around here'*.

The 14 step Lean Institutionalization Process that we have developed is described below.

1. Management education and commitment followed by engagement.

To implement Lean successfully, senior management must understand the process, and the benefits to be derived from the program. So often, we see management setting goals and expectations from Lean, and yet they have never had a moment of education. They may have heard about it, or seen the success that others have had, but they do not truly understand the process. This trend seems to be most prevalent at the more senior levels of the corporation. This leads to conflicting messages and metrics at review sessions.

As an example, many companies we visit still have the traditional 'productivity' metric that is used to measure performance. This can, and often does, lead to building inventory that is not needed in an attempt to meet or exceed the productivity goals. The cost associated with carrying inventory that has no immediate need is huge and should be avoided. In our previous lives, we had all kinds of mechanisms at our disposal to manipulate these numbers. Few of these were beneficial to the business, but they avoided the repercussions that followed low efficiency numbers. One of the key messages we preach in Lean is that inventory is 'evil'. This would appear to be at odds with the so-called productivity ratings.

There are many other examples of metrics such as machine utilization, earned labor hours, quality etc. that cause unwanted behaviors. How then can management reconcile the metrics required in a Lean environment with traditional metrics, and maintain a credible message?

The reality is that many of the traditional metrics must go, and they need to be replaced by metrics that enhance the Lean process. Senior management must get a solid Lean education and provide performance metrics that ensure the success of the Lean transformation program. In one large corporation where we have conducted training sessions, a significant amount of money, time and personnel resource has been invested in the Lean program. There is a Lean plan in place and the Lean process is being rolled out in various divisions. At the corporate level, however, management is still conducting review sessions using the traditional metrics and, as a result, there is real confusion and skepticism in the lower ranks about what the company is trying to accomplish.

When we talk about senior management, we mean all of them. We frequently find that some functions, such as accounting or sales, are not on board, and this impedes successful implementation.

Some senior managers are embarrassed by the thought of getting a Lean education, as they fear that showing a lack of knowledge will undermine the respect they receive. On the contrary, we have found that those who are committed and engaged in the process are highly respected by the other employees in the organization, as it shows that everyone is equally willing to learn and change.

In one of our training courses, a division president attended for six days, took part in all of the discussions and breakout sessions, and walked up to get his certificate at the end, just like everyone else. He told us that he had learned as much about his organization as he did about Lean, and he intended to participate in the next course also. From comments we received from other participants, his attendance was well received, and they learned much about him as well.

2. Management must clearly communicate the plan, the reason for it and, to the extent possible, outline the future following implementation.

We understand that it is not possible to predict the future; however, employees need to hear your best assessment of what the future holds. You must tell the truth, the whole truth and nothing but the truth; at least as you know it at the time. Nothing will kill this process quicker than lies, or subterfuge.

There is nothing worse than the environment in an organization that is constantly laying-off people. If downsizing is required, it is better that it happens quickly and only once. Any organization that touts Lean as a beneficial process and lays people off repeatedly is doomed to failure. Employees need to understand the compelling reason for implementing Lean, and how it will affect their daily lives.

There is no question that Lean frees up personnel. The productivity improvements are substantial, and you must decide what to do with the extra people. If you have natural attrition, or your company is growing, then it is easy to reassign people to new functions or not fill positions that have become vacant. Whatever your circumstances, be honest, and keep people informed. Remember, Lean success is entirely dependent on the *active* support of the workforce.

In one plant, people were aware that there was a plan in place to move operations to another location over an eighteen-month period. As you can imagine, nobody was happy about that. Nonetheless, the employees collectively implemented an aggressive Lean transformation. Today that plant is a shining star, and other operations are being moved into their facility. Any employee in that location will tell you that their survival, and current success, is due to Lean, and the honesty of management. They are happy that they had an opportunity to influence the decision instead of hearing about it when it was too late.

3. Policy Deployment must support Lean goals.

Policy Deployment is designed to ensure that everyone in the company pulls in the same direction, towards clearly defined and delegated goals. It is a critical part of any Lean implementation.

In many corporations, you will find that the objectives at the lower levels of the organization bear little, if any, relationship to corporate goals. Because Lean is a wall-to-wall transformation, it must be reflected in the objectives at every level of the corporation. It is only when everyone in the organization knows the priority that they can make decisions in line with the priority.

Business as usual is not a deployable policy. Priorities must be set with the intention of achieving the necessary change. Therefore, resources must be assigned differently. Objectives at every level must support the overall priorities, and be integrated to give one complete structure of aligned effort. Priorities should not be replaced every year. Instead, there should be an evolution. Everything we do in Lean is based on continuous incremental improvement.

Achieving Policy Deployment is not easy. It requires clear strategic direction on the part of corporate management, and an effective communication process to get the message to all levels of the organization. It will not happen by itself. It takes a great deal of work, and attention, but the result is worth the effort.

One company we worked with has a process in place to ensure that Kaizen events support the overall strategic goals. Their Kaizen events must be pre-approved to ensure they are in line with corporate goals. It is important to keep in mind that Kaizen will bring rapid and drastic change. If you have policy and procedure manuals, you will need to ensure you have a system to update those documents. Your ISO documentation in particular needs to be current.

There should be a reward strategy in place that is linked to achieving the priorities. This may be a bonus system, a profit sharing plan, or it can simply be the performance appraisal process.

4. Educate everyone in the organization.

Usually, when we talk about this subject, we get the 'deer in the headlights' look. A majority of managers do not see that we have spent years educating people on the way we do things now. Whether through formal, or informal, training we have institutionalized the processes we operate today. Yet, for some inexplicable reason, we do not want to educate everyone on Lean.

Most organizations have success when they implement Lean. However, some have seen significantly more than others. There is a direct correlation between the level of Lean education provided and the level of success attained. When we talk about education, we are not talking about pieces of Lean. We mean every element, every rule, and every tool.

We frequently encounter managers who tell us that they do not have the money to train everyone in the organization. In response, we say you do seem to have the money to continue to fund the waste that exists in your operations. Why not redirect those funds to a program of change? The bottom line is that waste has been budgeted, and approved, but there is no money available to fix it. This is typical of corporations who cannot see past next month or next quarter.

We are so emphatic on this concept that our company was formed to provide a low cost mechanism to train everyone in the company. We developed the Lean Mastery series of learning modules that are deployed across a company network, intranet or the Internet. They contain all of the Lean education that is needed and also have Power Point presentations, interactive forms and other tools to help people get up to speed quickly. Every form of learning is accommodated.

As we present these tools, we find that the budget saga is often just a ruse. The reality is that management just does not get it. If you think that you can have outstanding Lean success without investing in education, we wish you the best of luck.

An interesting aside note here is that European and Asian companies are far more receptive to using the latest technology to train employees than many American companies. Despite the cost effectiveness, many American managers cling tightly to the old concepts. They will spend $5,000.00 to send someone to classroom training but will not spend $5,000.00 to train the entire site workforce using the latest technology. There may be logic here, but we cannot see it.

5. Lean must be the only system allowed. A real culture change must take place.

Often we visit companies where one or two lines have been 'converted' to a Lean process, and others continue to operate in the traditional batch and queue mode, with little evidence that these remaining process will ever be converted. After touring these facilities, and discussing the Lean program with management, it is clear that, those who fear change are blocking the conversion. This is allowed to happen because management themselves are not committed to Lean or understand that it requires a rapid and drastic culture change. What kind of message do you think this sends to the workforce?

If you are going to implement Lean, then do it comprehensively. This process is a complete business transformation. Changing pieces of the operation simply adds confusion, and endorses the flavor of the month syndrome. When you have educated everyone in the organization, there is no need for this. People will come to you asking to get involved. All you have to do it get out of the way and let them proceed.

Another condition we see often is that companies will implement a few of the Lean tools such as SMED or 5S. They see Lean as some kind of menu from which to select. We can assure you that this does not work. In fact, for many companies, they have done this many times before. Many of the Lean tools are not new concepts. They have been around for many years, and companies have tried to implement them as stand-alone projects, with little success. Take Kanban as an example. For over twenty years, companies have tried to implement successful Kanban systems and have discovered that Kanban only works effectively in a Pull environment.

Some time ago, we received a request to provide a quote to a company who wanted to do 5S training. Our contact was somewhat indignant when we asked why they wanted to limit their improvement program to 5S alone. We also asked if the company understood that the total benefit and success of a 5S program was contingent upon understanding and applying all aspects of Lean. We declined the opportunity to provide a quote because we wanted to avoid the problems that will inevitably arise when you are limiting your focus to a single aspect of Lean. Our training materials are built around this theory of the total integration of Lean concepts, and we had no desire to expose ourselves to a contract that would be impossible to execute in terms of the customer's desired outcome. As an interesting side note, the company in question was prepared to spend a lot of money for the 5S training. The individual who contacted us had given us the range of prices that had been previously quoted. Without exception, these quotes exceeded our cost for an entire week of total integrated Lean training. When we educate on any single aspect of Lean it is difficult for us to ignore the need to integrate that aspect into Lean as a whole.

6. People must be given authority to make changes.

As human beings, we have a need for power. If you look around most companies, you will find that people have developed informal systems that give them a degree of control or power in their own work areas. As you implement Lean, and allow people to participate in Kaizen events, you should also allow them to implement changes. Do not be afraid of this. In all likelihood, the worst that will happen in a Kaizen event is that you are no better off than you are today. However, the vast majority of Kaizen events produce improvements, and allowing people to implement them develops a sense of accomplishment and ownership. Remember, if you do not give people power they will take it.

The power people take, if not given, is not as obvious as the power that comes with, and is exercised by, those who have positions of authority in an organization. One of the authors had an experience in high school football that might help explain this. A junior varsity quarterback with a real authoritarian attitude failed to comprehend the real power of the other ten individuals on the offensive team. After being battered severely as a result of a few strategically missed blocks, the quarterback finally got the message, and his attitude changed significantly. The deliberate act of refusing to participate, or perform, can be difficult to detect but can negatively affect your desired outcome. Power can be manifested by the failure to act.

7. Concrete heads must be removed.

In our Change chapters, we discussed the section of the workforce population that will be unwilling to change or participate in the Lean process. At some point, you will have to address this problem. These people are a negative influence, and can seriously damage your Lean initiatives. They need to be removed from the process.

The worst kind of concrete head is the 'Lean concrete head". We describe these individuals as so-called Lean champions, or facilitators, who are unwilling to listen to any other point of view. If Lean is truly a participative process, this cannot be allowed. One company we worked with had just appointed a Lean facilitator to direct the Lean program. This facilitator had never had any previous exposure to Lean. His appointment to this new position resulted from the significant success he had experienced in his previous job. We offered free time to help him to get up to speed but, unfortunately, he already knew everything. He would not listen to any guidance to help avoid the pitfalls. He had already decided how he was going to approach his new position, and had no interest in hearing anything different. Today, he has little support, and the Lean implementation is taking longer than it should. Nonetheless, his attitude has not changed at all.

8. Management must stay focused and understand the transition phases.

There is enough history of Lean implementation to understand that there are transition phases. Early in the Lean process, companies are likely to find a substantial amount of 'low hanging fruit". This can have a significant positive impact on financial performance. Some managers see this as an ongoing process, and plan similar results for future financial periods. Others see this as the end of the program.

The reality is that, after the low hanging fruit has been picked, the organization needs to transition to an aggressive continuous improvement mode. This will also have positive benefits, but the pace will be different. There is no limit to the improvements that can be made over time, and the improvement process should never end. Management must understand this, and stay focused. Many years ago, Brian had a boss who told him to prepare for the long haul, as the process he was working on was a marathon, not a sprint. This is also true of Lean.

9. Avoid Hysteresis.

In lay terms, hysteresis is a process that takes place when material returns to its original condition after the pressure has been removed. For example, metal will expand as heat is applied, and will contract once the heat has been removed. Organizations behave in a similar way. The pressure to become Lean must be maintained, or the organization will return to its former operating mode.

We have proven repeatedly that single piece flow works. Yet, we often see workstations, where we have successfully implemented this concept, with little batches of material lined up awaiting processing. The only reason those batches are there is because they are tolerated. The pressure to enforce single piece flow has been removed.

If, at any point, you accept failure to implement any part of the Lean plan, for any reason, you are giving the wrong message. People will view this as lack of commitment. Remember, Lean must be the only system allowed.

10. Tools applied to the whole organization.

Very often, we see Lean applied to manufacturing only. When we talk about Lean, we use the term Lean Enterprise and not Lean Manufacturing. While manufacturing is a good place to start, you cannot become Lean unless you apply the concepts to the complete enterprise.

If you fail to apply Lean concepts to the office and administrative areas of your organization, you are missing a huge chunk of the pie. In fact, you are missing the majority of it. You should begin administrative Kaizen events early in the implementation, and you should not exclude any department.

Applying Lean to manufacturing only permeates the 'we versus they' attitude that exists in most manufacturing companies. Lean is most successful in an environment where everyone is working together to achieve common goals, and where respect for individuals is inherent in the way things are done. Having different functions working together will bring down many of the barriers that exist in companies today. Besides, people from another function will often have the answer to a problem that has plagued you in the past. This is one of the reasons we insist that Kaizen teams are cross-functional.

Your Lean transformation plan should also require participation by supplier and end-customer personnel. The benefits attained by Lean companies we have worked with, that had involvement by supplier and end-customer participants, exceeded the benefits achieved by those who did not get them involved.

Suppliers will understand what you are trying to accomplish if they participate in your improvement program. They are quick to embrace the Lean concepts themselves, and are more likely to meet your Kanban system requirements when they improve their own processes. Customers will appreciate the process changes you are making, and will gain confidence in your ability to react to their changing needs. Subsequently, the demand for product from these customers can become linear and more predictable. Customers are quick to recognize that you are offering them the ability to reduce their investment in inventory and still meet their needs.

11. All improvements must be recognized.

Not everyone has the opportunity to land the big fish. You should be quite happy to receive many little fish instead. People will continue to work on improvement projects when they see that their work is appreciated. Recognition is the key to ensuring the preservation of the continuous improvement process. As human beings, we all like to be recognized, and appreciated. This has a significantly bigger impact than giving people money.

We should understand that small improvements add up to big gains. They say that if you improve 1% a day for seventy days you will be twice as good as you are now. While it is important to achieve the financial benefits that will accrue over time from small gains, it is also essential to understand the contribution that this can make to the culture change.

Recognition does not have to be formal, or even major. However, it does have to be genuine. Lack of sincerity will kill this process in a heartbeat. An honest pat on the back can have a longer-lasting impact than an impersonal public speech. You should also have a process in place that guarantees that you do not leave anyone out.

12. No embarrassment or retribution for admitting problems.

If we truly want to make improvements, we need to know what problems exist. Few managers have the time or level of involvement needed to establish every single problem that exists. Management needs to develop a climate where people can expose the problems that exist, without fear of reprisal. Too often we have seen situations where employees revealed problems in their own work areas only to be reprimanded by their supervisors for doing so. In these situations, people are unlikely to want the backlash that will follow future participation.

This is part of the management culture change that must take place. We all know these problems exist but may not know specifically what they are. The whole purpose of Lean is to get at these problems and fix them. Management needs to get over any insecurity, and get on with the job of eliminating waste. Frankly, there is no place for this kind of pettiness in any organization; Lean or not. Focus on the process and not the people.

13. Be innovative and creative.

We have seen outstanding examples of creativity in the time we have been involved with Lean. By nature, people are imaginative and innovative. Few of these creations have cost much money, and it is clear that we would never have arrived at such solutions, no matter how much time we spent at it.

Unleash this power, then stand back, and watch what happens. Given the opportunity, people will present ideas that may have been on their minds for years. They will also have ideas for solving problems in other areas that may surprise you. Once again, get out of the way and let them do it. What have you got to loose?

14. Make it fun!

We have never seen anything in writing that says conducting business has to be a miserable experience. We have, however, seen situations where laughing was frowned upon as it, supposedly, demonstrated lack of seriousness. If your employees are cheerful you will get positive results that will reach all the way to your customers. If you are uncomfortable with this, lighten up – perhaps you are the problem. The performance of the business is critically important, but you are likely to achieve that performance faster, and with a higher level of quality, if the workforce is content. You will achieve that by respect, and by having your employees involved; pure and simple.

We have seen many companies that have a plaque on the wall that says something to the effect that 'people are our most valued resource'. These plaques must be on sale somewhere as they mean about as much as they cost. If the quoted statement were true, you would not have to put it on the wall. Your employees would know it, your suppliers would know it and your customers would know it. Truly valuing your employees means that you believe they are the business. You have a vast amount of untapped potential at your disposal if only you would use it. When you reach this point, you will understand what fun in business really means.

Institutionalizing Lean is a key to success.

5

Lean Math

> Beware of little expenses;
> a small leak will sink a great ship.
> - *Benjamin Franklin*

By way of background each of us has over 30 years experience in finance and manufacturing operations prior to becoming Lean authors and consultants. Keith Gilpatrick held positions in public accounting; internal auditing; manufacturing administration; and manufacturing operations as a Director of Lean Manufacturing. Keith has lived and worked in Europe and was responsible for internal audit operations and acquisition audits there and throughout Europe, the Pacific Rim; South America; Mexico and Australia. As the Director of Lean Operations, Keith was responsible for over twenty separate plants in the United States, Europe, South America, Asia, Mexico and Africa.

Brian Furlong began his career in banking and moved on to manufacturing management. Brian has established; moved; and managed multi-site manufacturing operations throughout the world including the United States; Mainland Europe; Eastern Europe; Asia; Africa; and Central America. Brian also has acquisition and turnaround experience.

We have included the risks and costs associated with establishing foreign operations in this chapter because we know, from experience, that many of these are usually not anticipated when companies are planning a move.

In this book we use the expression Lean Math to describe the calculations and analyses that you should perform to determine potential margins from outsourced or offshore operations, as compared to the potential margins from a Lean transformation of your current operations. You might ask, "If my company is not Lean how can I possibly compare margins from Lean operations with those from outsourced or offshore opportunities?" That would be a fair question. As Lean Enterprise experts with experience in global manufacturing operations we would ask the following questions.

- How can companies make the decision to outsource, or go offshore, without first considering the margin improvements they could make through a Lean transformation?

- Exactly what costs are the companies, who are outsourcing or moving operations, using to determine the future margins from those operations?

- Are your accounting systems sophisticated enough to identify true product margins and report these correctly?

We use these questions to demonstrate that you could be far removed in time from the point in which you established your cost system, and conditions could have changed over the years that lessened the accuracy of the data being reported. As we recall, it was standard fare for someone in a manufacturing performance review to make some comment about the accuracy or fairness of the standard cost system.

In this chapter, we will examine the issues that should be considered when comparing your current operational costs to those of outsourced or offshore production operations. We will also address the cost of quality which we believe few companies accurately measure. Cost of Quality has a significant impact on business profits. Lean Enterprise concepts are powerful in helping to identify and reduce your cost of quality exposure, and provide real and significant margin improvement.

Outsourcing

Let's first consider outsourcing to companies located within the continental United States. Deciding to outsource products, sub-assemblies, or parts that you currently manufacture is, at the very least, an admission that your current process is too costly and can be performed more efficiently by someone else. This other company can make what you manufacture today with a profit on the sale, and you have the additional freight and handling costs. You might also have to increase your inventory of these items to take into account a longer lead time, or provide safety stock which will add additional costs. You must consider the following cost of quality questions also.

- Will you need to inspect the products that have been outsourced?

- What are the additional costs if your supplier cannot supply product on time or in quantities that you need?

- Will you have additional costs expediting supplier orders, or perhaps additional costs that you will need to pay expediting the manufacture and shipment of your final product because a supplier did not meet a deadline, or provide products that met your quality requirements?

- What are the costs for moving machines, tools, or dies?

- What are the costs for de-commissioning equipment or the layoff costs for employees?

- What are the additional costs relating to engineering support early on in the transition?

- How long will the initial (real or perceived) cost advantage last? Is there a point in time when the costs incurred with the outsource decision will be paid back, or will this be a moving target because of eventual supplier price increases, or internal costs that never go away resulting from the outsourcing maneuver?

How do you account for all of these possible additional costs? Few companies have the ability, or even require that costs such as those described here be accumulated and analyzed. These additional costs will simply be incurred and appear somewhere on the profit and loss statement. Who's providing financial feedback on these outsourcing decisions? You need to calculate and report the total cost associated with any outsourcing decision.

Let's look at outsourcing outside the continental United States. Take all of the costs mentioned above and add the following:

- +% increase in freight, duty, packaging, and handling

- +% increase in inventory levels for safety stock

- +% increase in inventory to accommodate the distance and replenishment time

- +% increase in quality costs

- +% increase in expediting costs, and the number of instances where expediting will be necessary

- +% increase in engineering support costs

- +% increase in relocation of machinery, tools, and dies

- +% increase for NAFTA payroll equalization (Mexico)

- +% increase in communication/administration costs

Add to these costs the financial, or logistical risks, associated with doing business with a supplier who is located in a country that does not have a stable government, or one where costs will fluctuate based on the political environment, labor unions, or legislative trends. The cost associated with the risks that you incur doing business in certain offshore locations are probably not possible to calculate, you just have to hope that nothing will go wrong.

ISO (International Standards Organization), which is relatively harmless in the United States, is one example where, internationally, the rules and regulations can impact the economy of doing business. In Europe for example, there are hard and fast rules for testing that have been legislated through the ISO organizations. We fought an unsuccessful battle with the ISO authorities in Germany and France concerning the testing of water meters. The testing time was dictated by the ISO rules that required the register that measures water volume through the meter make a complete 360 degree turn. We attempted to reduce the testing time, and increase plant productivity by testing the accuracy of the meter at the 180 degree point. We argued that the accuracy of the meter could be determined at any point in the register reading if the volume of water flow and register reading were consistent. The ISO authorities in both Germany and France would not consider the science of this proposal, they simply said that the rule was the rule, and they would not consider any alternative test.

At that time, the ISO authorities were not interested in the economic impact of their rules and regulations. Their narrow focus was product quality, their way, irrespective of the business impact. You need to be aware that you may not be able to work with your international supplier to reduce costs and improve productivity in the same way that you can in your own operation or with a domestic supplier.

Then there are obscure laws that you note only after you have committed yourself to doing business in a particular country. For example, in Hong Kong there was a law that said if a tenant in a leased building did not pay his rent on time, the landlord could remove and sell all, or any one piece, of the equipment in the leased space to recover the unpaid rent, regardless of any legal title implications. A regulation, such as this, could disrupt product flow from suppliers who have short term financial issues. While obscure, we point out, that there are risks with international suppliers that could be anticipated if you do your planning and due diligence correctly.

In some European countries, the labor unions are mandated by the local governments. We have found dealing with those organizations to be a very different experience from those in the United States. While we have probably lost track of the exact statistics, the principle rule in Germany was that there was a ratio of one union representative for every one-hundred employees. (The last time we looked they were discussing changing that to 1:75) Once elected, these union representatives do not have to work; they simply walk around and get involved in employee issues. We had a plant go on a mini-strike because we were in the company providing Lean training to management. The signs they held said "We don't want any American Systems in our Company". The worker's council in this German plant was not going to participate in the Lean program. A large number of the products manufactured at this plant are now being manufactured in Slovakia, and the jobs that the worker's council were trying to protect have been lost.

The political environment, and government mandated labor unions, can impact the flow of products. While your company may be subject to union issues in the United States, the problems that can arise with unions in foreign countries can be more complex and issues can take longer to resolve.

It is important to note that you should not approach offshore outsourcing as you would that of domestic operation. Be aware of the local rules governing business; and attempt to identify the total cost of that decision.

Establishing Offshore Operations

The reasons for establishing your own offshore manufacturing operations or establishing a partnership with an offshore company may vary. You may have a customer who wants you to move your operations closer to one of their international facilities; you may need to move manufacturing operations closer to an international market; or you may want to move offshore to take advantage of (real or perceived) lower manufacturing costs. For now, let us assume that a decision has been made.

Our direct experience with offshore moves, leads us to conclude that the decisions are usually made with only partial knowledge of the true cost of doing business in a foreign country; and that the total cost has been greatly underestimated. Unfortunately, you would be hard pressed to find an executive who would admit that mistakes had been made. In fact, there is a plethora of evidence that suggests that the executives involved in these decisions have sometimes gone out of their way to manipulate financial results to avoid making the obvious failures public. We have seen many formal requests for capital needed to establish, or participate in, foreign operations that were project based. These requests remained open for years, and far exceeded the original forecasted cost. Further evidence is derived from audits that reported hidden or misappropriated costs associated with the project.

Another interesting outcome of some of the offshore moves, or partnerships, we have been associated with is that the partner or management hired to run a subsidiary, were obviously much shrewder than our management. While we could probably write a separate book on this subject, suffice is it to say that in several cases U.S. corporate management figuratively showed up for a gunfight armed with a dull knife.

Some years ago, one of the authors was involved in a contract that a U.S. telephone company had received to install telephone equipment in Iran. The Iranian authorities negotiated late delivery clauses. The telephone company was happy to include these in the contract because they were sure that nothing would go wrong with delivery. What the telephone company did not consider was that the Iranian customs authority would delay the import authorization until the late delivery clause had been reached. The U.S. Company cried foul, but could not point to a provision in the contract that would exclude late delivery for this reason. What was really happening here was that the customs officials would release the equipment if someone showed-up with a bag full of cash to speed up the process. So, to avoid the late delivery charges, morning visits were made to the customs office with cash in hand. As an aside, the person transporting the cash each day objected to being escorted and the process didn't work at all unless they were alone.

If you are currently contemplating an offshore move or partnership, we caution you to do so intelligently. Do not accept a capital request that is prepared at such a high altitude that you can not distinguish the different types of costs that you will incur, or that you cannot recognize that certain inevitable costs have been excluded.

To begin with, you can assume that, at a minimum, the increased costs and risks that are associated with outsourcing will also apply in the case of offshore operations. Be sure to ask the financial and planning teams about those costs. Consider the following risks and costs that you might experience in an offshore operation.

177

Risks

In the spirit of the figurative gunfight, be sure that you are as prepared to do business as your foreign partner, or that you are assured of your capability to operate and manage a company that could be located thousands of miles from your corporate headquarters.

What is the labor cost and what will it be five years from now?

In many low labor cost countries inflation is a significant factor. A straight comparison between the current labor cost in the U.S. and the new country may appear to be advantageous. However, when projected out, it may be that inflation will quickly eat up the apparent advantages. You should review both the direct cost and the benefit cost.

What is the labor turnover rate?

A high turnover of employees will result in many unforeseen costs. There will be constant re-training and quality issues. It is important to understand what the turnover rate is and what the causes are.

Does the lower labor cost offset the additional transport and logistics costs?

Unless you are immediately planning to source everything locally (which is unlikely), you will need to take into account the additional logistics costs. These include such issues as transportation, time, export and import administration, brokers, duties and any special storage conditions. We will cover these issues in more detail later, but these costs, and the whole logistics effort, should be evaluated to determine that a real benefit exists.

Who will manage the operation; ex-patriot or local personnel?

The difference here could be significant and each offers its own opportunities for risks and unforeseen costs. A situation where temporary expatriate management is contemplated, with an eventual transfer to local management, could extend well beyond your initial appraisal, and add significant costs to the overall plan. This situation could add volatility that is not anticipated if the location is less than desirable, and you are not able to make the planned transition. We have observed many instances where ex-patriot management has been unstable because the organization needed to run an offshore plant could not be established using local personnel within the prescribed period of time.

Consider also that using local management personnel could offer its own challenges because there are bound to be differences in management or ethical philosophy between you and your host country. In some areas of the world, it is not uncommon that sporadic changes will occur in local supplier lists for reasons other than quality and price. In several cases, we have noticed that suppliers change immediately after there is a local management change. One could speculate as to why the changes occur, but it is very difficult to prove any hypothesis. These changes can be disruptive causing any number of problems in the future. Work ethics of management and employees in your host country is a variable that can add costs to operations that you simply do not experience at home.

It is our experience that the level of onsite support needed to provide good quality, and a predictable flow of materials, has been consistently underestimated.

What are your quality expectations? Are these expectations shared by local management and production employees?

Will any differences in the concept of quality add additional costs? We have observed many instances where the level of quality that was available in the domestic operation could not be met in the foreign operation without adding significant costs. As an example, we were involved in a quality issue with a subsidiary in China that was fabricating and assembling bodies for gas meters. Thousands of gas meters built at the China subsidiary failed to pass the U.K. regulatory examination once they arrived. After incurring thousands of dollars in travel and living costs to have engineers from the U.K. make multiple trips to China, the problem was traced to the failure to clean a plastic lapping machine to the specifications prescribed by the machine's manufacturer. Even after this requirement was expressed to local management, product continued to fail the U.K. test. Local management in China would not stop the machine to perform the required cleaning because it would affect productivity. In this situation, our Company was in partnership with the Chinese government and the Chinese manager would not lower the productivity expectation in lieu of the quality consideration. The solution was to hard wire a timer to the machine so that it would stop running at the same time each day, and not run again until the following morning. This, however, was not accomplished easily.

Another issue raised at this Chinese plant was that we had an ex-patriot manager who shared the management responsibilities with the local Chinese manager. Whenever the ex-patriot manager increased productivity for any one week the local manager would call a party meeting and the whole production facility would empty out. The Chinese manager did not want to make less than expected, but he did not want to make more either - because employment was a higher priority than profit!

How reliable is the transportation system in your host country?

Is the transportation infrastructure capable of meeting the challenges that can arise due to climatic conditions? We have seen transportation operations come to a standstill, or became erratic, during certain seasons, in certain areas of the world. If you are not aware of this, you could get caught with insufficient on-hand inventory to meet customer requirements, and incur huge increases in premium transportation costs as a result. These are not anomalies. Monsoons and severe winters are common in some so-called low cost countries. You may get product to the dock but what will the extra charges be if you want priority treatment?

Will you be able to transfer your technology or manufacturing process easily to your host country?

We have seen a number of cases where machines that were intended for use in an assembly process were cast aside, and manual processes put in their place. There were two scenarios where this could occur. The first was that there was no local expertise available to service machines that failed, and a manual process had to be substituted. Another reason for setting costly equipment aside was that local management simply felt that they could provide a manual process that would get the job done. This is not necessarily a bad situation. Providing a manual process for one that was intended to be accomplished using a machine is okay, if the quality and on-time delivery does not suffer. It is only a bad situation if you did not anticipate this and incurred to cost to export the equipment. Another important consideration is that you should not assume that equipment that can be operated in the U.S. will always work elsewhere without additional costs for human, operational or environmental considerations, etc.

As an example, Keith used to work for the manufacturer of the first electronic cash register. The product was state-of-the-art in America and the company quickly moved to market the product in the U.K. This turned into a financial disaster for a short period of time because the company failed to recognize the weight of British coins. When the U.K. owners of the new cash registers filled the registers with change, the spring designed to open the cash drawer was not strong enough and it failed to open. The design team in the U.S. had, however, considered the layout of the cash drawer to accommodate the larger sized paper currency. The cost of the retrofit was massive, and any profit made by the company on the original sale swiftly disappeared.

Another important consideration, that is usually missed, is that some countries will not allow the importation of machinery or equipment that is older than a specific number of years.

Other countries will prohibit the importation of items, such as shelving, if there is a local supplier that can provide this. Failure to understand these regulations can add unexpected costs and delays.

Be aware of factors such as water pressure and purity; reliable electrical supply; size, strength, and sex of the workforce; and other variables that can impact the proper operation of a production line or production equipment.

It might be difficult to associate a specific cost with the above mentioned risks. The idea is to consider these issues, and attempt to measure the risk/reward aspects of a move offshore. Can you operate offshore and expect to realize the quality, price, future price reduction, and delivery expectations of your customers?

Choosing a country

Questions about the choice of country that should be considered when contemplating or planning an offshore move of operations or a partnership with an offshore company include:

- Is the country of choice politically aligned with the U.S.? Are there friendly relations? Does it have most favored nation status?

- Is the country politically stable? Who is the opposition party, what are their philosophies and how likely are they to be elected?

- Is there any customer who will not accept product from your host country?

- Will the host country of any of your customers add high tariffs to products produced in your host manufacturing country?

- Are there any social or other standards that would make it difficult to do business in, or live in that country?

- Does this country have a history of nationalizing foreign companies or is there potential for this happening?

- Does the U.S have an embassy or consulate in the country?

- Is travel unrestricted?

- Does the country offer grants and incentives for foreign corporations and what are the terms?

- Is it difficult to get work permits/visas and what are the terms for renewal?

- Is there a good supply of educated people available for the labor pool?

- What are the language issues? Are there sufficient English speaking people available to have a bi-lingual capability available for key positions at least?

- Does the country allow for temporary importation of parts or subassemblies free of duty?

- What are the corporate, personal and property tax rules?

- Can dividends be repatriated and what are the terms?

- Is the local currency stable and can business be transacted in multiple currencies?

- What is the national inflation rate?

- Is there a sufficient supply of high quality suppliers to enable local sourcing of materials?

- What is the climate? Can this be harmful to your product; production equipment; or make it difficult to ensure that employees are in attendance?

- What is the time zone difference, and how will this impact communications?

- Are there opportunities in the domestic market, and what are the conditions for participating?

Choosing a specific location within the country you have selected.

Once the country selection has been made, there are a number of factors that will influence the selection of a location.

Important note: At the outset you need to engage an attorney who will provide the legal services you need to review contracts, permits, byelaws etc. You should never have the same attorney as your builder, property manager, or other key participants in the start-up process. Larger companies will have a legal department who can provide this service, or select a local attorney on your behalf. If this service is not available then take the time to select the right firm and check out all references. This may save you considerable cost in the long run.

The following is a list of questions you need to answer when choosing a location.

- Are there any local consultancy companies to help with start-up? Can they help you through the local company formation, import/export regulations, permits, hiring, bank accounts, housing, etc? Can they provide references? What is the cost?

- Are there pre-built factories, or offices, available that will suit your purpose? Can you lease, or do you have to purchase?

- If you have to build, is there available land, and is there a sufficient supply of quality architects and builders available to choose from. Do they offer lease plans and what are the terms? Will they handle all of the planning and permit issues?

- Are there utilities available? What is the cost of hook-up? How long will it take?

- What is the quality of local communications? Can you effectively operate telephone, fax, email and network systems?

- What are the local and national environmental regulations? Do your products and processes comply? When in doubt you should apply the U.S. EPA standards.

- Is there a university close by that can offer a supply of qualified, bi-lingual people for many different functions?

- Can people easily be trained to read blueprints, perform administrative functions etc?

- Is there a high turnover rate for labor? What is the reason? Can you compete effectively?

- Are there grants or incentives available from local government or development agencies for hiring or training?

- Are there any local taxes such as rates, property taxes, etc?

- Is there an airport close by with an adequate flight schedule? Is ocean transportation convenient and is there a connecting rail service?

- Is there good local transportation available for both people and goods? In many low cost labor countries people do not have access to cars and must use public or privately arranged transportation.

- Are there any other U.S. companies operating in the same area? If so, take the time to contact them, and enquire about their specific experiences operating in the area.

- Is there a local Chamber of Commerce or development agency that can provide a template for start-up operations?

When acquiring property through a lease it is important to fully understand the lease terms and conditions. These will likely outline the responsibilities of both the landlord and the tenant, and you should be comfortable with your obligations. If the building is new, be sure to obtain warranty certificates for major pieces of equipment such as air conditioners, furnaces etc as you will likely be responsible for their ongoing service and maintenance. You should clearly understand who is responsible for maintenance of the building, and who should supply services such as landscaping, trash removal etc.

Most lease contracts will contain an inflation clause and wherever possible this should be linked to the consumer price index (CPI) in the U.S. and not a local inflation index that may cause excessive increases in future years.

You should fully understand the implication of clauses for late payment and ensure that these are acceptable. These are often couched in language that is unclear, and your attorney should ensure that there will be no future surprises.

Most property companies will want to tie you to a lease for as long as possible. You should attempt to minimize the term of the lease, as unforeseen conditions may cause your company to make alternative plans after start up has been accomplished. At a minimum you should try to include some language in longer leases that allows you to get out of the lease, even with a penalty that amounts to less than the cost of the full term. That penalty should be scaled down over time.

All references to environmental compliance and obligations must be fully understood and agreed to. These have the potential to cause major financial problems later.

Finally, the lease will identify the country that has jurisdiction in the event of a legal dispute or arbitration. You should do everything possible to ensure that disputes are settled based on U.S. law. If this is not possible, your attorney should ensure that there are no potential future liabilities that may impact you.

Are you aware of the Cultural differences and the impact on your operations?

Understanding the cultural differences and neutralizing their effect will have a direct impact on the financial performance of the operation. While culture is not directly considered to be a financial aspect, a lack of understanding of it could result in lower than expected performance, work delays or stoppages, and quality problems.

Cultures generally fall into individualistic or collectivistic classifications.[1] This is useful information as it helps to make communication and performance more effective.

The key characteristics of each classification are as follows:

Individualistic	Collectivistic
"I" identity	"We" identity
Self realization	Fitting into the group
Independent	Interdependent
Say what you think	Avoid confrontations in a group
Emphasis on Individual goals	Emphasis on group goals
Communication direct, precise	Communication indirect, imprecise

---

[1] Reference: Experiencing Other Cultures by Sal Nunez

Countries that fall into each category are listed below.

Individualistic	**Collectivistic**
Australia, Belgium, Canada	Brazil, China, Columbia
Denmark, Finland, France	Egypt, Greece, India
Germany, Britain, Ireland	Japan, Kenya, Korea
Israel, Italy, Netherlands	Mexico, Nigeria, Panama
New Zealand, Norway, South Africa	Pakistan, Peru, Saudi Arabia
Sweden, Switzerland, United States	Thailand, Venezuela, Vietnam

Potential costs that may be incurred and should be anticipated include several factors mentioned below.

Documentation

Product documentation

If you are the manufacturing a product in a foreign country you may need to have the following translated. Please keep in mind that technical translations are best performed by people who have technical capability.

- **Drawings**: All drawings will need to be translated. At a minimum you will need to translate key words or measurements.

- **Procedures:** Manufacturing, test and quality procedures will need to be translated.

- **ISO-9000 Manuals**: These should be translated; as it is likely you will need to certify the new facility to this standard.

- **Instruction Manuals**: You may need to translate these if you plan on selling the products in the local market. If you plan to repatriate the products then this will not be necessary.

- **Sales and Marketing documentation:** If you plan on selling the products in the local market you will need to have the following translated.

- **Brochures:** Any sales literature that is used to explain or promote your products or services.

- **Product certifications:** If the products have been certified to any specific standards, you will need to be able to present these certificates in a format the customer can read.

- **Media:** Any videotapes, compact discs or other promotional materials will need to be translated.

Other Documentation

There are many other documents that may need to be translated. These may include accounting manuals, human resource manuals, corporate policies and procedures, safety notices, signs and a variety of different types of agreements.

Computer systems

Care should be taken to understand the reporting requirements from the new company, and how to interface these requirements with your existing database. You may want to link in by network, through the Internet or provide a totally separate system. Once again you need to consider what language will be used, and the logistics of passing data back and forth. Costs for computer hardware, software, and ancillary services should be included whether purchased or leased. Treating these as capital or expense will depend on your company's accounting policies. The cost of additional security controls also needs to be considered.

Potential costs:

- Communications infrastructure costs

- Communications monthly costs

- Travel costs

- Video conferencing costs

Translators

It is a good idea to hire the services of a translator who can help you to interface with customers, suppliers, government agencies etc. When hiring this person be sure to hire someone who can perform cultural translations, as well as language translations. This may save you some embarrassing moments during meetings or negotiations, and will prevent you from causing unintended offence. Do not be surprised if you attend some meetings to find that the person you are meeting with has his or her own translator also in attendance. In these circumstances you will find discussions heavy going but this is a fact of life in many places.

Daily correspondence such as email, faxes and phone conversations can be confusing even with bi-lingual personnel on board. When you are not in visual contact with someone it can be difficult to ensure that your intended meaning is fully understood. A good translator can be very useful in these situations.

Potential costs:

- Cost of translators
- Lost time
- Product quality costs

Quality/Training

One of the key difficulties with any new operation is achieving the quality standards necessary to avoid rework and customer returns. Training is an on-going process in new operations, and allowance needs to be made in the financial projections for this. The levels of training will depend on a number of factors such as turnover, levels of prior education, complexity of the subject to be learned etc. The ultimate goal is quality, and there are some hidden costs that may not be immediately obvious.

Very often the documentation in use in the domestic plant has been unofficially modified, or the employees simply know that it is wrong and make the necessary adjustments during the manufacturing process. If the documentation is not accurate passing it on to an offshore operation could expose you to quality problems.

There is a tendency in low labor cost countries to place additional people in the process to perform in process or final inspections. In most U.S. companies these practices have been eliminated, and the responsibility for quality placed on the workers performing the task. Even though the labor cost is low, adding extra people should be avoided if at all possible, and an extra effort put into training. More people in the process will cause hidden inefficiencies that translate into product cost that never seem to go away. Right at the outset, the quality standards expected should be clearly communicated, and no allowances should be made for accepting less than perfect product.

If the manufacturing process to be transferred has variability, then inexperienced people will compound that variability. Initial training will not eliminate the need for experience, and you may have to provide someone from the domestic operation to oversee manufacturing until the requisite experience level has been acquired. We are addressing known variability here where an experienced employee can judge that the quality levels are acceptable.

Processes that do not prevent variability will likely result in additional costs. Steps in the process that are open to interpretation are likely to be misinterpreted and result in additional cost.

Manufacturing steps should be mistake-proofed so that errors are not possible. It is worth the time and effort to do this. This prevents build up of incorrect product, or the possibility of receiving defective product back from customers.

Potential costs:

- Training

- Documentation verification

- Legal

- Lost time or quality cost due to variation

- Expatriate costs

- Write off of defective inventory

- In process or final inspections

- Higher product return costs

Expert Advice

As mentioned earlier, it is important to get good legal help at the beginning. While this is a start-up cost, it can prevent significant consequential costs by getting all of the legal aspects of the project done correctly.

Also, it is unlikely that project managers will have the necessary legal knowledge, or skills, to maneuver through the maze of rules and regulations that need to be followed.

Most major corporations will have a legal department that can provide assistance, or find a local attorney that they trust. In any case, you will need to secure this service, and check out all references. It is worth making some inquiries or phone calls to ensure you have a capable firm. Apart from the fees of the attorneys, there will be costs related to company start-up, securing licenses, permits, visas and a myriad of other fees that may need to be paid to the government, agencies, planning authorities, customs and perhaps some suppliers, or other institutions in the form of bonds or guarantees.

When selecting an attorney, find someone who has done this before, and who can provide you with an estimate of expenses related to that particular country or locality. Because most project managers have little legal knowledge, this is one area where non-budgeted costs will arise. Finding a firm with the necessary experience can prevent this. It is important to have good English versions of all documents and when the document is legally binding it should state that the English version will be used in any legal disputes or arbitration. Have these documents reviewed by your legal department to ensure nothing has been overlooked, and that the terms are acceptable. If this requires an extra expense it is worth it to guarantee peace of mind.

If this is your first venture into a country, it is possible that you will be asked to provide corporate or other guarantees for high cost items, such as lease payments, because you have no credit record. These requests may come in the form of a corporate guarantee, and you will likely be asked to produce certified accounts that clearly demonstrate your ability to pay. Larger corporations tend to want to provide those guarantees from the lowest possible entity and it can be difficult to provide certified accounts at that level. You may have to negotiate this point; providing corporate published accounts while providing the guarantee from a lower level entity.

If a bond is required, you will likely have to make a down payment of 10% or more to secure the bond. Bonds are often required for lease payments, customs authorities, major suppliers and any other large payments where the credit terms do not require immediate payment. You may wish to keep your legal firm on a retainer for some time to ensure that their services are available when required. Normally, this is not required but you may feel it is necessary depending on the size and complexity of the project.

Operations that have environmental issues may wish to retain the services of an attorney that is experienced in this area. This may be a different attorney from the one hired to perform your normal commercial services. Obtaining environmental permits can be an intricate process in some countries. Adherence to environmental rules and regulations is very important and there are requirements for maintaining records on emissions, spills, storage of hazardous substances etc. In the event of any dispute you will need a knowledgeable attorney.

Environmental clean up is a major cost item and it is wise to perform an environmental study that is accepted by the authorities prior to signing a lease or purchasing a property. Even if the environmental regulations in the country are weak at the start of your operations the laws could change during the time you are in operation. It would be wise to employ the standards set by the U.S. Environmental Protection Agency if the country standards are less than that.

Your attorney should be questioned on the legal requirements to comply with local labor laws. These are very often different to the laws in the U.S. Issues that might result in discrimination lawsuits in the U.S can often be non-issues in another country. For example, in some countries it is perfectly legal to advertise a position where both the sex and the age of the required applicants are clearly identified. In some countries, there are certain services you must provide for employees that you may not have to provide domestically. Examples here would be a company nurse when employment reaches a certain level or the provision of condoms to female employees in countries where population control is an issue.

If the proposed new operation involves a partnership with a local company that is providing technology, or special information that is key to your success, it would be wise to come to an arrangement that allows you first right of refusal in the event that the partner wishes to sell his or her piece of the business. This protection is necessary for the continued success of the business.

Corporate obligations may not always be on the radar screen of a project manager whose primary responsibility is to get an operation up and running. However, this is an important subject and has significant financial implications if it is not handled properly.

Potential costs:

- Attorney fees

- Permits, licenses, visas etc

- Translations

- Bonds, guarantees etc

- Escrow fees.

- Environmental studies and surveys

- Employee services

Technology

Your company's technology may be embedded in the product (service) or the process. It is important to protect that technology, and to do everything possible to ensure that your foreign partners or employees do not become your competitors. You can do this by patent, or by having non-compete or confidentiality agreements signed. This should apply to employees, suppliers, and customers where you are revealing capability or data that would accommodate a competitive start up operation.

This is particularly important if your new operation is a sub-contract arrangement with a local manufacturer.

It is essential that you maintain strict design control. Failure to do this could result in product or process problems. Changes need to go through the same types of processes that would exist in the domestic operation, or you may wish to maintain all design control at the domestic location.

When sourcing parts locally for your production process, you may run into problems if your products contain parts that are in imperial measurements and the new country is metric. You may not be able to locate the parts you need and shipping items such as fasteners etc can be very expensive. Similarly, your design group needs to pay attention to items such as voltage and frequency which are different in many countries.

There may be alternative, less-expensive materials available in the new country that may appear to be equivalent to the materials that you are currently using. A decision to change should not be left to the local purchasing people, as this may affect product performance. Items such as metals, plating, electronic components etc. need to be thoroughly verified before they are used, as the raw materials used in those parts may not be the same as the ones you are currently using. If appearance is important, then such items as paint mix or compound consistency may be an issue. Finding local sources for materials is beneficial as these materials may cost less, and there is considerable savings on transportation or logistics. However, the design group needs to be involved to verify that the substitutes are acceptable.

As we mentioned earlier, product drawings and vital equipment operating instructions need to be translated. For manufacturing it is important to have product, assembly, or process safety notices translated into the local language. You should use internationally recognized logos, or warning labels, throughout your operation.

In some cases you may only be setting up an engineering function in a new country where there is a ready supply of qualified, inexpensive labor. In this case it is important to ensure that your engineers recognize that new products and processes or technology developed by them are the property of the company. Patents should be taken out immediately when warranted.

When transferring technology (including software or code) to an overseas operation you need to ensure that you are in compliance with all U.S. Department of Commerce regulations on exports. You may have to get permission or acquire specific export licenses in certain circumstances. This requirement should be investigated long before decisions are made, or action is taken that would place your company in a position of non-conformance.

Shipments of products from your new location may be governed by the same regulations that would apply if you were shipping from the U.S. Contact the Department of Commerce to ensure that you understand the rules, and make certain that you are in compliance at all times.

There are strict regulations governing the export of technology, and failure to comply has serious consequences.

Your technology may be the barrier to the entry of competitors into your marketplace, and you need to pay the necessary attention to protecting it, and to complying with all regulations.

Here is a quick story regarding import tariffs or other costs associated with importing products. One of the authors was associated with a company that had a contract for parts with a Japanese manufacturer which stated that any difference in price relating to currency fluctuation would be invoiced separately, on a quarterly basis. The duty paid on the imported parts was based on the invoice that accompanied the shipment. It was noticed that there were several invoices paid by the company which represented additional costs because of currency fluctuations and that the related duty charges were not paid. By admitting these duty omissions and paying the duty on the currency fluctuation invoices, the company avoided fines that could have amounted to more than the cost of the original products. The point we wish to make is that the participants in a contract negotiation are rarely involved in the everyday operation of your business, and certain aspects of the contract may require administration that may be overlooked, and could subject your company to heavy fines.

Potential costs:

- Non-disclosure, non-compete agreements or patent approval

- Export compliance

- Translation

- Verification of alternative materials

Supply Base

We have already mentioned having a good local supply base for the purpose of saving cost, time and inventory. We also discussed the need to protect your technology against unauthorized use.

If your company has an existing supplier qualification program it is a good idea to extend this to the new location. Supplier audits should be carried out to ensure that the new supplier has the ability to provide acceptable quality; consistently. Consistency is very important, and this cannot be judged by samples alone. Samples often receive special care and attention, but the ability to produce on a regular basis can only be verified by an on-site visit.

Another benefit to on-site visits is to verify that the supplier does not indulge in labor practices that would be unacceptable to the company. In some cases it may be necessary to audit the sub-contractors that your primary supplier uses to ensure that the same rules apply.

Until you are comfortable with the performance of your new supplier, you may want to perform on-site verification of parts before they are shipped.

Where supplies are critical, it is wise to perform a credit check on the suppliers, or to verify that there is sufficient cash flow to maintain a steady supply of parts.

It is important to lock in the cost of parts from a new supplier so that you are not subjected to low bids just to get the business. Parts that are subject to variation in pricing because of market commodity prices need particular attention. Contracts should reflect prices that go down as well as up when commodity prices change. This may seem obvious, but many companies only pay attention when prices are increasing.

Suppliers need to operate to the same standards as you do when it comes to profitability and cash flow. However, they may be so eager to get new business that they do not fully understand the implications of accepting your terms. Considering the time it takes to find new suppliers, it is in your interests to point this out to them at the outset.

Take the time to make sure that each party, the supplier and you, understands the division of responsibility when it comes to quality. Where quality is visually interpreted as opposed to tested (painting, plating etc,) make sure the supplier has samples that reflect the only acceptable standard. This can be used for comparison prior to the supplier shipping parts. This will save considerable time, and the expense of shipping product back and forth.

Do not over-commit on quantity, as material specifications or product designs often change. Ideally, you want just in time supply of parts with a lead-time that allows your supplier to meet your needs in periods where demand may fluctuate.

Finally, make sure your documentation is accurate and legible so as to avoid any misunderstandings. The last thing you need is to have the supplier make parts to your specifications if those specifications are incorrect. This is not an uncommon situation. We have seen many situations where product quality issues have been ultimately traced to incorrect documentation at the customer location. It is also important to ensure that the supplier has the most current drawing revision level.

Potential costs:

- Supplier audits and visits

- Documentation verification

- Credit and financial checks

- Translation

Logistics

This section deals with the issues surrounding the transportation of goods to and from the new facility and the storage of inventories. Depending on your shipping method you will need a variety of paperwork that may be new to both your domestic and your foreign location.

Your traffic departments (in both locations) need to be familiar with all of the Department of Commerce regulations on exports, and you will need to ensure that you have the necessary export licenses. Some potential customers or even your potential partner may be on the Department of Commerce "denial listing" and you need to be aware of that.

Most of the established import/export brokers are aware of this and have processes that would protect you, but the ultimate responsibility is yours and you should be vigilant in this regard.

For transportation purposes, you need to be familiar with Airway Bills and Bills of Lading. Failure to complete these properly will result in delays. You will also need to complete commercial invoices and, where applicable, hazardous materials documentation.

You will likely need the services of a customs broker at each end to clear your goods, and you will have to comply with customs regulations in each country. Each customs authority has its own rules and regulations. Failure to comply with these regulations will result in delays, very detailed inspections, and even fines. Initially, you will receive a great deal of attention. If everything is in order, then over time you will only be subject to occasional inspections.

Be aware of the documentation, labeling and marking requirements of each customs authority and ensure that you comply. These may appear minor but are most often the reasons for delays. Country of manufacture labels will be required on products imported into the U.S. and you will need to fully understand the terminology that is allowed when applying the label describing this.

Make sure that the descriptions of your products do not cause unnecessary attention. Seemingly innocent descriptions can warrant undue attention, and you may need to provide greater clarification. Above all be truthful, as the consequences of doing otherwise are severe.

Also make sure that the quantities and actual items shipped match the paperwork. These quantities are used to calculate duty liability and will be checked from time to time.

Customs authorities are independent of any desire that a country may have to promote trade. If you give them a reason, they will become an unwelcome part of your everyday life. Compliance is a much easier route to take despite the fact that the requirements may appear cumbersome.

If the foreign country has a duty drawback system, you need to fully understand how it works. Customs will likely want to see a mechanism for tracking parts temporarily imported, and may want to see your added value calculations. You may be subject to unannounced audits. Depending on how the drawback system works you may need to maintain separate records that can be used to substantiate later claims for refunds. Do not be surprised if refunds take up to a year or even more.

U.S. customs will likely want evidence of exported parts being re-imported and the added value applied in the foreign country. In both cases bonds and company information may be required prior to trade commencing. Your products may be subject to deterioration in certain conditions such as cold, heat, humidity or moisture. You will need to ensure that they are packaged to withstand these conditions, if they are encountered. Insurance is an important consideration when transporting goods and you will need to investigate the type and cost of coverage you require and what deductible you will accept. Some companies are self-insured and will have a blanket policy with deductibles already specified.

If you are trading overseas you need to be familiar with the international set of trade terms called "INCO terms" that have been adopted by most countries. These will specify the responsibility for transportation and insurance costs and the liability between the customer and the supplier. Some transport companies may refuse to collect transport costs from your customer if they have had difficulty in the past, or if they are in a country that has foreign exchange restrictions or volatility. In those cases you may have to accept terms that you would normally not agree to. Consider also, that if you are shipping directly from your foreign location to a domestic end-user, your customer may not be willing to accept the additional transportation costs.

Depending on the country, you may need to trade with letters of credit. These require strict adherence to their terms, and failure to comply *exactly* with their wording may result in non-payment. Seemingly insignificant things like misspelled words can cause major problems. There are costs associated with the establishment and confirmation of letters of credit that are imposed by the bank. It is recommended that letters of credit be drawn on, and/or, confirmed by a US bank.

There is a significant amount of documentation and attention to detail required when transporting goods between countries. You will need experienced and knowledgeable personnel, and you will need the services of established, respectable customs brokers. Delays in transportation, due to errors, can result in significant additional production costs. Sufficient time should be allowed for all the necessary steps to be completed and this will likely result in a permanent in-transit inventory cycle. Sourcing product locally is clearly more cost effective provided you can achieve the necessary cost and quality targets outlined in earlier chapters.

Potential costs:

- Customs Brokers

- Duty

- Insurance

- Transportation

- Bank charges for letters of credit, etc.

- Bonds

- Storage

- Export licenses

- Record keeping for drawback.

The message we have conveyed in this section is that any executive contemplating outsourcing, or offshore operations, should do so only after his or her organization has supplied them with accurate financial and risk data. While time may be short, comprehensive preparation is necessary for such a critical decision. A Lean Enterprise transformation should also be considered as an alternative option. Challenge your organization to compare the costs of outsourcing, or offshore operations, to those that could be attained by eliminating the waste that exists in your current operations. The time required to organize, plan, and execute an outsourcing or offshore option could be used to implement Lean. You may find that you have a completely different view of the costs and a viable alternative.

Once a decision has been made to move an operation offshore, you should make sure it is a Lean operation. Go Lean before you make the move if at all possible. Implementing Lean in some cultures is a real challenge and may require a very different approach to the one you would use domestically. Make sure your new operation does not become an Elusive Lean Enterprise

Cost of Quality

Few companies can provide accurate financial data regarding their cost of quality. Does your company look at the financial impact that quality has on operations? Can your company distinguish between product quality and process quality costs? What do you know about your total cost of quality, and would a first-pass estimate of those costs be anywhere close to your actual costs? The cost of quality has been imbedded so deep in the profit and loss statements of most companies that the executives of those companies have not been able to recognize the magnitude of their problem. Few, if any, of the quality costs disappear when you elect to move operations offshore or source products from offshore suppliers. The same applies to decisions made to outsource products or services domestically.

Examine the following list of quality related costs and ask yourself if you know what the impact of these costs are on your profit and loss statement. Few companies establish programs to reduce these types of cost because they have accepted them as a cost of being in business.

Those companies that are seeking a Lean solution will reduce, if not eliminate, a substantial number of these types of quality costs. As you review this summary of quality costs ask yourself why you would want to continue supporting a quality philosophy that accommodates rather than resolves problems. The Cost of Quality alone should be a compelling reason to want to go Lean.

What metrics can be used to measure the elements of your cost of quality? Those listed below are the ones most commonly reported by companies today.

- Warranty and product recall.

- Scrap

- Rework and re-operation

- Inspection and appraisal

- Quality management and overhead

A majority of the above costs are already reported in the management accounts or operations reports.

The following are the cost of quality categories:

Category	Reason
Prevention	To avoid things going wrong
Appraisal	Things might go wrong
Internal Failure	Appraisal showed things did go wrong
External failure	Customers discovered things did go wrong.
Exceeding requirements	Providing something nobody needs
Lost opportunity	Market discovered things keep going wrong

Let us look at an explanation of each category.

Prevention costs

The cost of any action taken to prevent or reduce the risk of error or defect. For example: Training.

Appraisal Cost

The cost of evaluating the achievement of quality requirements. For example: Testing.

Failure Costs

Internal Failure Costs: The cost arising from errors or defects such as scrap, rectification, retesting, re-inspection and re-design before the product or service had seen delivered to the customer.

External Failure Costs: The costs incurred upon discovery by the end customer that the product is defective or does not meet current specifications.

Costs of exceeding requirements

The costs incurred when providing features, information, or services that are unnecessary or unimportant or for which there is no real requirement. Examples: Extra copies of documents; Reports that are not read; Over-engineering; Over-specifying or adding complexity.

Cost of lost opportunity

The revenue lost when existing or potential customers are lost when we fail to deliver quality product when it is needed. If quality costs are difficult to asses in your domestic operation, the problems will be compounded when you move that operation offshore.

At the back of this book, in Appendix I, there is a checklist in each category that can be used to help determine the true quality costs of any operation. The primary purpose of this Lean Math chapter was to point out that there are costs and risks associated with outsourcing or moving offshore if you are contemplating either option. We deliberately made our examples simple to point out that it can often be a small problem that brings you to your knees. The difficult problems are usually well known, and are the primary focus of most plans. As a final note; do not underestimate the importance of understanding the culture from both a cost and an operational perspective.

CHAPTER

6

Lean Enterprise and Six Sigma

**No one is more definite about the solution
than the one who doesn't understand the problem.**
- Robert Half

O ne amazing phenomenon that we have encountered is
the vying for stature between Lean Enterprise and Six
Sigma. Those who favor one, have a tendency to look
down on the other. Corporations today are under consistent
pressure to improve financial performance, and return greater
shareholder value. In markets where the opportunity to
increase price is limited, or non-existent, companies must look
to their cost structures and operating philosophies to improve
revenue growth.

Parts of this chapter were adapted from reference materials from Break-
through Technologies Inc. and Rath & Strong.

Lean Enterprise and Six-Sigma are powerful and complimentary strategies that can be used to identify and eliminate waste, improve quality, and improve financial performance. If improved financial performance is truly the goal then you will find that Lean and Six Sigma are necessary partner programs. If there is some kind of status battle going on, then the true goal needs to be clarified and reinforced.

Companies should use every tool available to put themselves in an unassailable position. Frequently, we encounter situations where Six Sigma personnel have been assigned the responsibility of evaluating or implementing Lean. In some instances, there is an air of snobbishness associated with this. The potential for Lean is not fully appreciated because it does not have the same lengthy learning curve as Six Sigma, and is therefore regarded as a lesser program. In reality, the simplicity of Lean is what makes it so effective. Everyone can participate in a Lean transformation, whereas, in practice, Six Sigma has a tendency to be restricted to 'qualified' personnel.

We often hear that Six Sigma is a big company program. We counter that by saying that Six Sigma, like Lean, is a process improvement program, and should be used where there is a need. Implementing Lean Enterprise can contribute significantly to the success of the Six Sigma program. When used together they can produce outstanding results.

In this chapter we will examine how Lean and Six Sigma can work together. We will show how implementing the Lean elements, rules and tools can contribute to Six Sigma success. Six Sigma and Lean use many of the same tools and have the elimination of waste as their goal.

Six Sigma Defined

Six-Sigma is a process, and a philosophy, for achieving zero defects. It is a business initiative that uses data and statistics to drive factual decisions, and it applies to all company processes. Six-Sigma helps to develop continuous incremental improvement as a core competency.

What is a Sigma ?

Sigma is a letter in the Greek alphabet. The term "sigma" is used to designate the distribution or spread about the mean (average) of any process or procedure; in other words, the variation. For a business or manufacturing process, the sigma value is a metric that indicates how well that process is performing. The higher the sigma value, the better. Sigma measures the capability of the process to perform defect-free work. A defect is anything that results in customer dissatisfaction. With Six-Sigma, the common measurement index is 'defects-per-unit,' where a unit can be virtually anything - a component, a piece of material, a line of code, an administrative form, a time frame, a distance, etc. The sigma value indicates how often defects are likely to occur. The higher the sigma value, the less likely a process will produce defects. As sigma increases, costs go down, cycle time goes down, and customer satisfaction goes up.

Six-Sigma is a term that means a defect level of only 3.4 parts defective out of every one million opportunities. At first, achieving Six- Sigma may seem impossible. Many companies strive to give their customers only 1% defects and consider this good performance. However, we have come to expect much better in our daily lives. Consider the following approximation of what 1% defective means:

- 32,000 babies dropped in the delivery room every year.

- 15 minutes of unsafe drinking water every day.

- Two short or long landings at most major airports each day.

- 20,000 lost articles of mail per hour.

- 5,000 incorrect surgical operations per week.

- 200,000 wrong drug prescriptions per year in the USA.

- 240 defective parts in the average new car.

- No electricity for 88 hours every year.

As consumers we would be unwilling to accept the performance outlined above, and have come to expect significantly higher quality. Companies on the leading edge are also striving for significantly higher performance, and are translating that into financial gain.

What is a process?

A process is a set of operations that are performed to achieve a desired result. Processes can be used to make a product, develop a product, render a service, or perform an administrative task. In a domestic environment, a process could be the act of getting dressed, or cutting the grass. In a business environment a process could be the assembly of parts, mixing of compounds, or responding to a customer enquiry. Most processes contain inefficiencies, or variations that can lead to cost, time, quality, or customer service problems.

What causes defects?

Defects are typically caused by excess variation due to inadequate manufacturing, or administrative process capability, supplier material variation, or unreasonably tight design specifications that are outside of the requirements of the customer. Six-Sigma focuses on eliminating the variation.

Lean Enterprise and Six-Sigma

Lean Enterprise, and Six-Sigma are complimentary strategies that focus on improving processes, and achieving zero defects. When implemented first, Lean Enterprise concepts, such as Kaizen, will transform operations so that waste is eliminated, and process variations are reduced. This allows limited Six-Sigma resources to focus on solving the real problem. For example, by implementing the "Standard Work" rule of Lean Enterprise, variations in the way a product is manufactured can be eliminated . Problems may remain that result in poor yield, and Six-Sigma tools can be employed to identify, and solve those problems. Six-Sigma training is extensive. Typically, fully qualified personnel are in short supply, and when they are available they are needed to work on real problems as opposed to working on symptoms. Six-Sigma focuses on building quality into the products, and the processes to achieve consistent zero defects.

You need to be familiar with Six Sigma to understand how these two programs can work together. If you are not familiar with Six Sigma, an overview follows.

Six Sigma Overview

The Six-Sigma approach to process improvement is five-phased. There is a logical link between each phase, and both the previous and next phases.

Define - During this phase the purpose and scope of the project are defined. A team is formed, and given a charter that will define the assignment, and the estimated dollar impact. A clear statement of the intended improvement is required. The defects should also be defined at this stage, and a process map developed. During this phase leadership approval for the project is received.

Measure - In this second phase, information is gathered about the current situation. The process has been mapped, and inputs and outputs identified. Baseline data is gathered on current process performance, and the factors that are currently influencing the problem are identified. The capability of the measurement system should also be assessed. At the end of this phase a more focused problem statement should be developed.

Analyze - The purpose of this phase is to identify the root cause of the problem. A Failure Mode Effect Analysis (FMEA) should be performed. FMEA is a structured approach to identify the ways in which a product or process can fail by estimating the risk associated with specific causes; prioritize the actions that should be taken to reduce the risk; and evaluate the design validation plan for a product or the current control plan for a process. The primary purpose of FMEA is to identify ways the product or process can fail, and to eliminate, or reduce, the risk of failure. The cause should be identified, and confirmed with data. A plan should be developed at this point for the next phase.

Improve - The purpose of this phase is to experiment and implement solutions that address the root cause of the problem. Critical inputs will need to be verified, and optimized. At the end of this phase there should be verified actions that eliminate, or significantly reduce, the impact of the root cause.

Control - The objective of the control phase is to implement a plan to control, and continuously improve a process. Solutions are evaluated, and the process is standardized. Results and recommendations should be documented as well as all findings.

In the following sections each of these phases is explained in more detail.

Define

In this phase, project goals and limitations are defined using strategic objectives and customer needs. Some of the tools used during this phase are as follows:

Charter Definition

This is a statement of the team objectives to provide clear expectations, and responsibilities. The charter should include the scope of the project, the financial or improvement deliverables, and the responsibilities of team members. As the project proceeds, and more information becomes known, the charter may have to be reviewed, so that it becomes more clearly focused.

Stakeholder Analysis

As the project is likely to bring about significant changes to a process it is important to rally support, and buy-in, from the stakeholders. These would be department managers, internal and external customers of the process, suppliers, and support departments such as Accounting or Design Engineering.

It is critical to establish effective communication with the stakeholders so that better solutions are identified, and pitfalls are avoided.

Process Map

A process map is a graphical illustration of the process. It will be used to identify all value added, and non-value added, process steps. It will identify key process inputs and outputs. Supplier and customer data should be included.

Typically, quality is judged based on the output from a process. The quality of the output is improved by analyzing input and variations in the process.

The results of process mapping is data that identifies where measurement studies are required, data that shows where the control plan needs improvement, and data that defines what is critical to quality.

Rolled Throughput Yield (RTY)

RTY is calculated by multiplying the yield at each process step as compared to looking at the yield from final test in the First Time yield method. RTY is a more accurate reflection of what is actually happening in terms of quality, and it exposes problems that may otherwise be hidden.

Customer Value

This is a critical component of many facets of Lean Enterprise and Six-Sigma. Knowing what the customer really wants, and what is perceived as value is key to:

- Identifying critical product or service specifications.

- Knowing where to focus improvement efforts.

- Deciding what products or services to offer.

- Knowing what constitutes customer satisfaction. Knowing what represents value to the customer will also help to highlight non value-added activity.

At the end of the define phase of the project the following should be available:

- Clearly defined goals that show what must be accomplished.

- Who the team members are and who the stake-holders are.

- Project limitations in terms of finance, time, and personnel.

- A process map showing detailed process steps, and both value and non-value added activity.

- The Roll Through Yield.

- Clearly defined customer specifications and value.

Measure

The objective of the measure phase is to locate the source of the problems as precisely as possible. This is accomplished by gaining an understanding of existing process conditions based on factual data. During this phase, a baseline is also established to measure process performance capability. The following are some of the tools that are employed during the measure phase.

Data Collection

At this point it is necessary to collect data. You must decide what data to collect, and how that data is measured. The data collected will relate directly to what you want to accomplish, and this, in turn, will lead to how the data should be analyzed. It is important to ensure that data that is collected is consistent across different time periods, and different operating conditions. You must be aware of any variables, or inconsistencies, that have been introduced.

Data collection is typically very time consuming so it is important to identify the key measures, and to clarify objectives. The goal is to ensure that the data collected gives the information, or answers you need. Data collected needs to be prioritized and funneled.

Prioritization helps to identify the small number of important variables that need to be measured, and analyzed, and helps to keep the data collection efforts focused. This is done by linking output variables to customer requirements, and by linking input and process variables to output variables. Prioritization should include the following:

- Listing all output variables.

- Ranking of output variables.

- Listing all input and process variables.

- Correlation of the relationship between output variables, and input, or process variables.

Failure Mode Effect Analysis

Failure Mode Effect Analysis is useful during the data collection phase, as it can be effective in focusing the data collection activity on the variables that are critical to the process. It should be used when there is there is confusion on what the important variables are, and how they affect output.

FMEA does the following:

- Documents effects of critical inputs on critical outputs when critical inputs go wrong.

- Documents the causes of critical inputs going wrong.

- Documents a control plan for preventing, or detecting, causes.

- Provides prioritization for actions, and documents the actions taken.

Cause and Effect Matrix

This is a Quality Function Deployment matrix (QFD) that stresses the importance of understanding customer requirements. It relates the critical inputs to the critical outputs (Customer Requirements) using the process map as the primary source. Critical outputs are scored as to importance to the customer. Critical inputs are scored as to relationship to critical outputs.

The outcome of this exercise is a Pareto of critical inputs to evaluate in the FMEA control plans. It also provides input into the Capability Study step and provides input into the initial evaluation of the Process Control Plan in the control phase.

A number of other data collection, funneling and validation techniques can be used during the measurement phase. These would include Pareto charts (80/20 Rule), Frequency charts, Statistical Process Control, Stratification etc. Whatever mechanism is used it is important to ensure that the measurement capability is validated.

Measurement Capability Validation

Once the data has been collected, funneled and prioritized it is important to validate the measurement system. You need to determine the measurement capability for the critical outputs and inputs. This is sometimes referred to as Gage Repeatability & Reproducibility (Gage R&R). A gage R&R is a set of tests to assess the repeatability and reproducibility of the measurement system. When several people measure several units several times, the variation is analyzed to determine how much of it relates to the people, how much to the procedures or techniques or how much to the parts.

There are five steps to verifying that a measurement system is accurate.

- **Step 1**- Accuracy results when the value measured has little deviation from the actual value. Accuracy is usually verified by comparing repeated measurements to a known standard.

- **Step 2**- Repeatability is defined as the variation between successive measurements of the same part, same characteristic, by the same person using the same instrument.

- **Step 3**-Reproducibility is defined as the difference in the average of the measurements made by different persons using the same or different instruments when measuring the identical characteristic.

- **Step 4**-Stability relates to measurements taken by the same person in the same way under the same conditions.

- **Step 5**-Device Capability is when there is sufficient resolution in the device used to measure so that it can observe different values within the range of product variation in the previous steps.

Process Capability

Defining process capability involves statistical measures that summarize how much variation there is in a process relative to output specifications. The ultimate objective is to have a process that can produce zero defects. A defect is described as anything that results in customer dissatisfaction, anything that results in non-conformance, anything that causes an individual to deviate from the normal process, or anything that prevents the output from meeting the requirements of the customer. Process capability is determined by use of Process Capability Indices.

These indices are used to:

- Measure the capability of a process relative to the process specifications.

- Provide a single number to assess the performance of a process.

- Provide the capability to compare the performance of different processes.

- Prioritize improvement efforts.

To increase the capability of a process it is necessary to decrease the process variation. This, in turn, results in greater predictability, less scrap, rework or wasted effort, products that perform better or higher quality service levels, and ultimately satisfied customers.

Process Sigma

Process Sigma is the capability of the process relative to the specifications for that process. Results are measured in Defects Per Million Opportunities (DPMO). This is a measure of actual total product quality because it allows prediction, analysis, planning, and benchmarking by the process improvement team. A key to successful use of DPMO in eliminating defects is to capture DPMO by causal area. Focus by Pareto analysis on the largest contributors to defects and then drive them to zero.

Defects Per Million Opportunities, can be used in benchmarking because it is standardized to provide an equivalent comparison of products or services of varying complexity (e.g. telephone compared to a fighter aircraft).

At the end of the measurement phase you should be in a position to define the problems that are occurring and under what conditions they are likely to occur. You should be able to demonstrate how critical inputs and outputs were selected and prioritized, and what has been done to validate the measurement system. At this point it is likely that the data is showing patterns or trends. Finally you should know the capability of the process.

Analyze

The purpose of this phase is to develop theories of problem root causes, to validate such theories with data and to finally select the real root cause. Once a problem has been selected you need to create a list of possible root causes and then organize those to see the potential relationships between cause and effect.

A number of different tools can be used in the Analyze phase. The following is just a sample.

Brainstorming

This technique is familiar to most people and has been around for some time. Nonetheless, it is very effective in generating many ideas to identify root causes in a very short time. During a brainstorming exercise, creativity is encouraged, and people feel free to say whatever comes into their minds. Criticism of ideas is not allowed, and momentum is gained by piggybacking other ideas.

Five Whys

This techniques is used extensively in Lean Enterprise during Kaizen events and other problem solving activities. It is a method of getting to the root cause of problems. The theory is that the first reason given for why something didn't work is rarely the real root cause reason for failure. This tool is particularly useful during Kaizen events where the majority of the team is not familiar with the process. Every step in the process should be challenged, and the 5-why method is a great way to get the job done. After a very short period of time everyone will use this method to validate not only the work others are doing, but they will also look at what they do and ask why.

Cause and Effect Matrix

See previous section.

Hypothesis Testing

Hypothesis testing facilitates the proper handling of uncertainty. It minimizes subjectivity and encourages the questioning of assumptions. It helps to prevent the omission of important data and it reduces the risk of decision errors.

Hypothesis testing is the process of taking a practical problem and translating it to a statistical problem. A hypothesis is a statement that something is true. For example, if we get ' heads' eight times out of ten coin flips we may say the coin is fixed in some way. There is a small probability that we can be wrong, but we're willing to take the chance.

Hypotheses are tested in business the same way; we attribute very unusual events to causes rather than pure chance. The question is whether differences between samples, processes etc. are due to random cause variation or whether there is a real difference.

There are a number of other tools that can be used during the analyze phase such as regression analysis, design of experiments, multi-vari studies, central limit theorem, chi-square etc. The intention here is not to provide detailed information on the analysis tools but rather to show that there are various techniques used to analyze problems. At the end of the analysis phase you should be able to show the likely causes, which causes will be investigated further, and why you will investigate them, what data was collected and how that data was interpreted.

Improve

In this phase, we should be ready to develop, implement and evaluate solutions. The objective is to show, based on data, that the solution(s) solve the problem and that improvements are achieved as a result. It is important to develop a cost/benefit analysis for each potential solution to ensure that the selected remedy can be financially supported by the organization. There is no point in defining and implementing solutions that are cost prohibitive, and that will later be rejected. If there are a number of possible solutions it is important to get consensus on which solution to pursue, and to test that solution through a pilot run. Getting consensus is a process of reaching the best decision through the involvement of everyone on the team. It is not simply a vote but rather an opportunity to hear, understand and evaluate all opinions. Each member of the team should be able to understand the final decision and why it is the best likely solution. That is not to say that everyone will be fully satisfied with the decision made but everyone should fully support it, and be prepared to see it through to conclusion.

The next step is to conduct a trial or pilot run to corroborate the expected results, and to ensure that the solution is a practical one. The trial will highlight any unforeseen problems and risks, and will help to bring about ownership from the stakeholders. The trial will also highlight where training is needed, and indicate areas where controls need to be put in place.

There are a number of different tools used in the improve phase. Many of them have been mentioned or described previously.

Brainstorming, FMEA, Hypothesis testing, Data Collection

See previous section.

Design of Experiments

Design of experiments is a systematic series of tests in which various Input Variables are directly manipulated and the effects on the Output Variables are observed.

A well designed experiment eliminates all possible causes except the one that you are testing. If an effect occurs on the Key Process Output Variable, then it can be tied directly to the Key Process Input Variable's you have directly manipulated and not to some other variable. Experiments are used to:

Characterize a Process

- Determines which inputs most affect the outputs.

- Includes controllable and uncontrollable inputs.

- Identifies critical process and noise variables.

- Identifies those variables that need to be carefully controlled in the process.

- Provides direction for controlling inputs rather than control charting the outputs.

Optimize a Process

- Determines where the critical Inputs should be set.

- Determines "real" specification limits.

Assist Process Design

- Helps in understanding inputs early in the design process.

- Provides direction for "robust" designs.

There are different types of experiments:

- Trial and Error
- One-Factor-at-a-Time (OFAT)
- Fractional Factorials.
- Full Factorials.
- Response Surface Methods.
- Others.

At the end of the improve phase we should be able to; specify the solution(s) selected, specify the criteria used to select the solution(s), specify how the solution(s) relates to the cause(s), show the results of the trials or pilot runs and detail the plans or implementing the solution(s).

Control

In this final phase, we need to ensure that we have the controls in place to ensure that the problem does not recur, and that we have a continuous improvement process in place. The reason that controls are put in place is to ensure that we consistently operate our processes in such a manner that output meets customer requirements consistently.

The objective of an effective control plan is to:

- Operate the processes consistently on target with minimum (or preferably no) variation.

- Eliminate process tampering.

- Assure that the process improvements that have been identified and implemented become institutionalized.

- Provide for ample training in all procedures.

- Include required review or maintenance schedules.

The following are the components of a control plan:

Process map steps

- Key process output variables, targets & specifications.

- Key process input variables with appropriate tolerances and control limits.

- Important uncontrollable inputs.

- Capability analysis results.

Control methods and tools

- Statistical Process Control (SPC) - a set of procedures for identifying and responding to out-of-control points and undesirable trends.

- A variety of control charts to ensure on-going monitoring of the performance of the process.

- Automated process controls.

- Checklists to ensure that critical actions are completed.

- Mistake proofing systems (Poka-yoke) to ensure that errors are not possible.

- Standard operating procedures and procedures required to react to out-of-control points.

- Workmanship standards to show the quality of work required.

- Sampling and testing systems to verify quality.

- Measurement capability analysis (see earlier chapter).

- Training

- Total Productive Maintenance (TPM)

To maintain effective control we need to validate the results and ensure that any changes comply with operating policies. We need to train everyone involved with the process and provide user-friendly documentation for future reference. It is important to implement tools such as SPC to ensure that the process remains in control and that there is immediate (and preferably audible and visual) notification if it goes out of control. Wherever possible we should use mistake proofing to eliminate the possibility of error. Systems should be put in place to ensure that preventive action is taken so that machines are in peak operating condition or equipment is properly calibrated. Process steps need to be standardized to eliminate variation and changes should only be permitted when data shows that a better method has been identified. Finally, we need to ensure that the stakeholders buy into the solution and have them involved in continuous improvement.

At the end of the control phase we should be able to show how the actual results compared to the planned results. We should have sufficient data to demonstrate that the solution should be standardized. Documentation should be in place to support the new process and it should be easy to use. We should identify what controls have been put in place to ensure the process remains stable and what actions are required should the process go out of control. Finally, there should be data to indicate that future improvements are recommended and a plan to accomplish them.

Six Sigma key participants with a description of their roles.

Champions

These individuals are the drivers of the Six-Sigma program and typically select and track significant improvement projects throughout the organization. Champions will ensure that selected projects meet the organization's strategic goals. To support their roles, champions will identify individuals in the organization to become process improvement experts. These individuals will be trained and certified in Six-Sigma methodology, and will become known as Green Belts, Black Belts or Master Black Belts.

The differentiation between Green Belts, Black Belts and Master Black belts lies in the level of training and the amount of time dedicated to the Six-Sigma program.

Green Belts

These people receive approximately two weeks of training and dedicate approximately 25% of their time to improvement projects within their area of responsibility. Green Belt candidates are typically selected from individuals who have lead recent improvement projects, have problem solving experience, who are results oriented, and who are respected within their current discipline.

Black Belts

Black Belts receive approximately four weeks of training and dedicate all of their time to improvement projects that are greater in scope. Black Belt candidates are selected using the same criteria as Green Belts

Master Black Belts

These individuals are Black belts who undergo an additional two weeks of advanced training and all of their time is dedicated to project consulting, project support, administration and training. Candidates for Master Black Belts come from existing Black Belts who have demonstrated that they have mastered the Six-Sigma problem solving techniques, and who have the aptitude for training and consulting. These individuals should be comfortable working at all levels of the organization.

Certification

Green Belts and Black Belts must meet the following criteria to be certified.

- The required training has been satisfactorily completed.

- A project has been completed that demonstrates proficiency with the tools and techniques taught during training.

- A project report has been completed and certified by a next level Belt demonstrating that the required level of expertise has been attained.

- Black Belt certification requires that three months of savings on at least two projects be demonstrated.

Following certification, Green Belts should complete at least a one year tour of duty and Black Belts should complete at least two years.

Responsibilities

Green Belts/Black Belts

- Use Six-Sigma tools and techniques to assure maximum possible benefit from selected projects and ensure projects are completed on time.

- Work with team members and others to collect data, ensure process understanding, and implement improvement actions.

- Co-ordinate with champions to ensure that there are no barriers to progress.

- Identify new projects that can yield significant improvements.

Master Black Belts

- Perform analysis of strategic opportunities so that specific projects can be defined.

- Provide training for Black belts and Green Belts.

- Assist with projects that are outside of the scope or ability of existing resources.

- Provide guidance, assistance or coaching for individuals or teams that need it.

Champions

- Ensure an adequate number of Green and Black Belts are trained to accomplish the business goals. Assign tours of duty and replace personnel who have left the program following the completion of their assignments.

- Monitor projects to ensure desired progress is being made and barriers removed.

- Deploy resources to projects in order of priority.

- Work with all personnel to ensure a continuing supply of savings opportunities.

- Review progress with senior management and communicate the status of projects to all employees.

Six Sigma Project Selection

In order to ensure limited Six-Sigma resources are effectively used it is important to select high-quality projects.

The following criteria should be used in project selection.

- Project tackles a problem that significantly impacts cost or productivity.

- It addresses an issue which impacts the customer.

- Has documentation based on a reliable measurement system.

- The impact can be seen on the bottom line.

- Prior attempts to resolve the problem have failed.

- Problem can be tackled as is or can be broken down into related smaller projects.

Projects can be selected by using one of the following methods.

Strategic

Strategic projects are those which have an impact across many facets of the organization and impact the overall success of the business.

Operational

These projects have been selected by a champion (but can be nominated by anyone) from within their area of operation, and should contain significant savings opportunities. This should involve approval of a project steering committee to validate the opportunities, and ensure that resources are correctly prioritized.

Project Tracking

Champions should review projects on a monthly basis to assess performance and to determine whether the expected savings can be achieved on time. During this review the champion should address issues which may negatively impact the achievement of the project objective. Where necessary, the champion should request assistance from senior management to remove roadblocks.

From time to time it may be found that a project is no longer valid because the original assumptions were incorrect or because conditions have changed to the point that there is insufficient remaining benefit. If this happens the project should be cancelled immediately and the Six- Sigma resources reassigned to a more lucrative assignment.

When a project has been completed it is important to recognize and celebrate the success. However, completed projects must include documented evidence of the achievement of the project goals and must contain data demonstrating on-going control of the process as well as any additional future actions that may be required.

Lean with Six Sigma

Earlier we outlined the Lean Enterprise Elements, Rules, and Tools. In the following sections there is a discussion on how the application of these Elements, Rules and Tools can lead the way, and eliminate many of the variables that would be encountered by a Six-Sigma expert. By using Lean Enterprise to identify and eliminate these variables, the Six- Sigma expert can focus on root cause problem solving.

Six-Sigma and Lean Elements

Value

Knowing exactly what the customer perceives as value will help a company reduce the level of dissatisfaction. Lean Enterprise requires a restatement of customer perceived value. In traditional batch-and-queue manufacturing operations, value can become distorted and be focused more on the short-term tactical goals of the company. Providing and applying resources that are of no value to the customer is wasteful, and the associated costs are not recovered from the customer.

Over-engineering a product can cause high manufacturing and assembly costs, create difficult assembly routines, and require in-process or final inspection effort. It is likely that your customer will not recognize the value of these products and will seek a lower cost alternative to your product.

If products are designed to meet the perceived value of the customer and result in production assembly procedures that are easy to perform, the total costs of manufacturing those products can be reduced and overall quality will be higher.

Improvements to product design and assembly techniques that arise from a Lean Enterprise transformation can greatly reduce the variations, and improve the product quality. This alone may eliminate the need to have a Six-Sigma expert involved.

Value Stream

Lean Enterprise requires that the systems used to provide value to the end customer or downstream customer of an upstream process be understood and include only those processes that provide value. To accomplish this, every system involved in the delivery of value to customers must be examined. The Value Stream map is used to depict the flow of value through these processes. The value stream mapping performed as part of the Lean Enterprise transformation can eliminate both waste and variations in processes that would ultimately be examined by a Six-Sigma expert. These process maps would assist in the information gathering stage of the Six-Sigma process.

Flow

Lean Enterprise transforms batch-and-queue manufacturing processes into one-piece-flow processes that can eliminate a major portion of the quality issues and related costs that result when product is manufactured in batches. In a one-piece-flow manufacturing process, quality issues that arise can be detected earlier in the process and require less rework. Attempting to determine where a quality issue originated using Six-Sigma techniques in a batch-and-queue process will be more difficult and certainly take much more time. Fool proofing techniques that are employed when transforming batch-and-queue to one-piece-flow will also eliminate a substantial number of the quality issues that might otherwise require a Six-Sigma expert to detect.

Pull

Manufacturing only when there is a customer order can also reduce quality costs. Product that was manufactured in advance of a customer demand could be defective, and the longer the time between manufacture and detection of quality issues, the more difficult it is to determine the root cause of the problem, and the process itself will be more costly. It is also more likely that more than one customer will experience the quality issue when defective product is shipped from a finished goods inventory.

Perfection

Lean Enterprise constantly seeks perfection in everything that a company does. This is accomplished by implementing the previously mentioned Elements and providing a method for continuous process improvement. Continuous improvement is accomplished using self-directed teams of employees who have been trained on Lean Enterprise concepts to review all processes, eliminate waste, and strive to meet customer perceived value requirements. This program, which, in Lean Enterprise, is called Kaizen, is the vehicle used to implement all aspects of the Lean Enterprise transformation. Creating a workforce that is continually conscious of eliminating waste and providing value can be a powerful adjunct to a Six-Sigma program. Creating a culture within a company where value is constantly being defined, and quality is a top priority, can make the life of a Six-Sigma expert much easier and can add value to the program in general.

Six-Sigma and Lean Rules

Standard Work

As mentioned earlier, Standard Work can create processes that are less likely to contain variations that cause quality issues. When Flow is created in the production process, Standard Work instructions are prepared and production employees are trained to conduct Standard Work. Operator in-process inspection is a part of Standard Work. Operators are taught to inspect what they have done before passing material or assemblies on to the next process. The goal of Standard Work is to eliminate process variations and to eliminate the need for costly technical inspections at the end of the production process. Implementing Standard Work can eliminate a substantial number of quality issues that the Six-Sigma expert might otherwise have to contend with.

Reduce Material Travel

Lean Enterprise requires that the distance that material and sub-assemblies travel be limited. Reducing material travel saves time and can also reduce the probability that material and assemblies could be damaged during transport. This can help Six-Sigma personnel by eliminating quality problems.

Reduce People Travel

Lean Enterprise requires that the distance that hands and feet move be reduced. The reduction of hand and foot movement can save time and reduce the quality issues that can arise when production operators are required to make excess movements during the production process.

Variations in the assembly process can arise when there is substantial hand and foot movement. Operators will try to create ways to make the work easier to perform, and may not maintain Standard Work requirements. Any changes to Standard Work should be accomplished as a result of a Kaizen. The elimination of any variations will help Six-Sigma personnel to get to the root cause much faster.

Place the responsibility for the Lean education at the lowest level in the organization

Lean Enterprise requires that all employees be trained, and that the responsibility for that training be placed as low in the organization as possible. If the responsibility for training is placed at the lowest level in the organization, the company will be more likely to succeed in implementing a new culture. Having a workforce that is conscious of Value and Waste will have a beneficial impact on your Six-Sigma program.

Six-Sigma and Lean Tools

There are a substantial number of Lean Enterprise Tools that will be beneficial to the Six-Sigma program.

5S Programs

5S programs can have a very positive impact on the attitude of employees. As a general rule, once a plant or administrative work area has undergone a 5S program the employees have pride in their work area and will want to maintain a high level of cleanliness. If 5S is introduced early in the Lean transformation, it provides a signal to the employees that management is committed to Lean and that changes are going to be made.

5S, properly implemented, can also have a significant impact on quality issues that might otherwise arise in a plant that is not clean or well organized. The job of a Six-Sigma expert can be made easier if your plant is clean and well organized.

TPM Programs

A program for machine and tool maintenance that extends the useful life of equipment, and ensures that equipment will be available when needed to produce product. A good TPM program will include maintenance procedures for all equipment operators as well as production cell workers (Autonomous Maintenance). TPM should include scheduled preventive maintenance. A TPM program can eliminate quality issues that might otherwise appear when equipment is not maintained properly. The elimination of quality problems is a primary goal of Six-Sigma.

Single Minute Exchange of Dies (SMED)

Single Minute Exchange of Dies, or quick changeover techniques that will reduce the size of batches processed by large machines that currently have complicated tool and die changeover requirements.

SMED can help eliminate quality issues that arise from producing in large batches and therefore help with the Six-Sigma process.

Process Mapping

Process Maps are process flow diagrams or charts that depict each step in a process as well as the number of people in that process and the numbers and types of documents currently used to control the process.

Process Maps are also useful to the Six-Sigma experts in the information gathering phase of the Six-Sigma program.

Line Balancing

Line balancing **is** a program where each process step is timed, recorded and presented on a frequency chart with the intent to balance the work so that each process step takes about the same amount of time to complete.

When balancing a production process, it is likely that process variations will also be identified and eliminated. The elimination of process variations will have a beneficial impact on product quality. Eliminating process variations during the Lean Transformation will also benefit a Six-Sigma program.

Poka-yoke (Error-proofing)

The primary purpose of Poka-yoke is to prevent costly inspection and rework, and to make the end product friendly to the user. As mentioned earlier, fool-proofing production processes can eliminate variations that cause quality issues. This is a primary goal of Six-Sigma.

Autonomation

Autonomation is using people in concert with machines to error-proof a process. Catching problems early in the process prevents costly rework or customer service issues. This is also the goal of Six-Sigma.

Design for Manufacturing and Assembly (DFMA)

DFMA is a design engineering theory and techniques that are used to ensure that the final design will assemble easily, and will be made using fewer parts that are readily available at the best price.

Using DFMA and mistake proofing-techniques can prevent problems from arising in the first place. This is the ultimate goal of Six-Sigma also.

Visual Workplace

The visual workplace can benefit the Six- Sigma expert by providing information regarding the current status of the process. Current problems are posted as well as other data relating to scrap or rework, and equipment availability.

Takt Time

For the Six-Sigma expert, knowing that a line has been balanced and is operating comfortably within Takt Time can eliminate certain problems that are known to exist in processes where production is rushed, and the work is not balanced. The balanced line operating to Takt Time is also required to perform Standard Work. The combination of Takt Time, balanced lines, and standard work provide an environment that is less likely to have variations that cause quality issues.

Five Why's

This tool is also used by Six-Sigma personnel.

One-Piece-Flow

Implementing this tool can help to detect quality problems (a goal of Six-Sigma) early in the process and prevent costly rework.

U-Shaped Production Cells

In the typical straight-line production process there are large distances between machines and people that create piles of inventory which often contain quality problems.

The U-shaped cell, operating single-piece-flow helps to eliminate this. Each of the tools above can help to eliminate variables that a Six-Sigma expert would undoubtedly encounter during a project and therefore save a considerable amount of time. This is valuable because Six-Sigma resources are usually limited and should be dedicated to projects that require their special knowledge.

Having undergone the expense of training your Six-Sigma personnel make sure they are doing meaningful work. Black Belts are in high demand and can easily be snapped up by another company. In one location we worked at, the Black Belt was the first one called upon to fix printers, fax machines etc.. That individual quickly realized that his talents could be used much more effectively by another company, and resigned.

The following are the keys to success for combining Lean and Six-Sigma.

- Incorporate Six-Sigma into the Lean Enterprise plan.

- Focus on balancing production lines, and establishing flow and pull systems prior to the implementation of Six-Sigma.

- Provide Lean Enterprise training for new hires with Six-Sigma expertise, or provide Lean training for employees who will receive Six-Sigma training in the future.

- Establish a cadre of Six-Sigma and Lean Enterprise facilitators as quickly as possible.

- Have Six-Sigma professionals involved in the development of Standard Work, TPM program development and assessment, 5S program assessments, DFMA programs, and participation in both manufacturing and administrative Kaizen events.

- Continuously seeking perfection.

When used in conjunction with Lean Enterprise, Six-Sigma provides companies with a powerful competitive weapon. Companies can streamline operations and processes to eliminate waste and provide the highest possible quality while focusing on customer value. Together, Six- Sigma and Lean Enterprise help to ensure that only value-added activities are performed, and that those activities generate high quality output consistently. Six-Sigma contains all of the tools necessary to define, measure, analyze, improve and control problem processes.

Companies that are implementing Six-Sigma and Lean Enterprise are seeing significant financial benefits while making radical improvements to processes and customer service levels. Typically, companies experience lower cost, higher quality, improved cash generation and higher customer satisfaction levels. Employees of those companies are more involved, and have a high degree of job satisfaction.

Lean Enterprise concepts and tools are used by everyone in the organization to eliminate waste, reduce variability and add value.

Six-Sigma requires dedicated professionals who are trained in the tools and techniques of root cause problem solving. By the nature of this training, the amount of available resources is limited, and these resources should be used wisely. Six-Sigma personnel should be employed in all aspects of an organization's operations from Marketing to Design to Accounting to Manufacturing. Anywhere there is a process there is an opportunity for improvement and Six-Sigma has the tools to facilitate that improvement.

Do not allow the existence of both programs to confuse you. They each have a critical role to play, and each should be viewed for the contribution it can make. When Six-Sigma is seen as some kind of superior program that supersedes Lean, there is a huge opportunity lost and the Lean Enterprise becomes elusive. When Lean is implemented, the Six- Sigma process becomes more effective.

Six-Sigma is a convincing process to identify root cause problems, to analyze those problems and to put controlled solutions in place to ensure that they do not recur.

The objective of this overview was to provide an outline of the capability of Six-Sigma when used to solve root cause problems. Many of the tools require detailed explanation and only a sampling has been covered here. More detailed Six-Sigma training is required for use by full or part-time Six-Sigma professionals.

This overview was also designed to show the critical role that Lean can play in making Six-Sigma more effective. When Six-Sigma only is selected, the opportunities for savings can be limited.

7

Lean in a Non-Manufacturing Enterprise

A company's business would increase 50% if you cleared the conference room of chairs.
- W.F. Henning

So far, we have focused heavily on manufacturing. Earlier when we presented the eight types of waste, we stated that each waste category was applicable to administrative processes as well. Regardless of the primary activity of your company, implementing Lean elements, rules, and tools via Kaizen is an effective way to improve margins and provide value to your customers. You can apply the elements of Lean (Value, Value Steam, Flow, Pull, and Perfection) in your service business.

The processes that dictate the quality, cost, and speed of the service of non-manufacturing businesses suffer from the same waste issues as those in manufacturing companies. Elaborate systems and processes have been created and deployed that do not always provide value to the downstream, or end customer. Moreover, many of these take significantly more time than they should.

There is a significant and critical difference between products and services when it comes to customers making value decisions. The frequency of customer value decisions can be much higher in service industries.

If you purchased an automobile and are not completely satisfied with your purchase you will probably not buy that make of automobile when the replacement time arrives (three to five years). Likewise, in terms of frequency, would be appliances, entertainment equipment, furniture, power tools, and lawn and garden equipment. You make decisions regarding banking, health care, insurance, and financial services numerous times in a single calendar year. This places service providers under constant pressure to offer the best, at less, and in a timely, convenient, and user-friendly manner.

The need for process improvement programs in a non-manufacturing enterprise was demonstrated, over a year ago, when one of the largest financial services companies announced that it was adopting Six-Sigma as a process improvement/quality program. According to an employee of that company, the need for speed could not be satisfied by the processes currently in use. Response time throughout the enterprise was considered the ultimate value that customers wanted.

While Six-Sigma can certainly be applied to a non-manufacturing process, it is more expensive as a solution to process problems than Lean. We would like to think that the company that chose Six-Sigma as a process improvement program did so without the knowledge of Lean. We can only repeat an earlier comment that the promotion of Lean, as a solution for all types of enterprises, has been lacking.

As we have stated, Six-Sigma is a powerful tool that works well in conjunction with Lean. Because of the costs associated with implementing a Six-Sigma program, we believe implementing Lean first, and reserving the more complicated problems for Six-Sigma, is a more effective way to change your business processes. The variation that a Six-Sigma specialist would detect in an administrative process can also be found by a Lean expert.

The primary reason for suggesting that Lean is a better solution is that Lean aims to change the culture of the enterprise. Six-Sigma does not attempt to change the culture. There are several other key points regarding the implementation of Lean versus Six-Sigma.

- The budget necessary to train twenty Six-Sigma experts might far exceed the total five year Lean transformation budget.

- You will spend so much money training a Six-Sigma expert that you will not want that person doing anything else, and you will likely have to replace that person once he or she leaves his or her regular job.

- Lean educates everyone in your company to become a process improvement expert.

- The costs to train twenty Lean facilitators could be half the cost of training one Six-Sigma expert.

- The Lean facilitator can be trained and will be training other employees and conducting cost saving Kaizen events long before a Six-Sigma student finishes his or her training.

The attrition rate for Six-Sigma experts can be high. You may have to pay your Six-Sigma experts much more than they previously earned to keep them. In one company where we worked many of the Six-Sigma black belts left the company soon after they had their first projects completed.

The Value element of Lean is no more difficult to get at in a service company than it is in a manufacturing company. The ultimate goal is to define value in the end customer context for every service product that you offer. If your end customer is not paying you to perform a process step, then you should consider eliminating that step. Service industries can be subject to third party reporting and regulatory requirements which must be performed, but add no value. Try to reduce the time and cost of participating in these mandatory programs.

Once you have defined value, you need to map the process that you use to deliver that value. Then you must make every attempt to eliminate all of the non-value-added process steps. Value should flow at the signal of your end customer. The common goal for every employee must be to seek perfection in everything they do.

The rules of Lean also apply to the processes that are used to deliver service. Create standard work for every process step in an effort to eliminate variations, and ensure that the process itself is of high quality, and is repeatable. Data and people movement should be limited and performed only if required by the downstream process, or customer. Every employee in your service enterprise should receive a Lean education, and be expected to participate in the implementation program.

The types, and frequency, of variations in administrative processes are much greater and can be difficult to police. The complete assembly instructions for a finished product in a manufacturing department can sometimes be displayed on a single sheet of paper, or one computer screen. The instructions for administrative processes can require many pages and involve more cross functional activity. There are many things that can change, or go wrong, over time in administrative processes:

- Policies change, and the changes are not communicated in a timely manner to either the external end customer, or internal administrators.

- The sub-cultures in the enterprise can result in failure to comply with certain operating policies.

- Ownership of problems can be contested when cross-functional interactivity is involved. Problems take longer to resolve at the expense of the end customer.

- People can make their own value decisions, and not perform a process step, or perhaps add their own which can add confusion and extend the process time.

- Both minor and significant IT systems changes, or enhancements, can cause short term process problems if they are not implemented properly.

- Customers can interpret process changes incorrectly, or not be aware of changes.

- It can be difficult to prove that a process step requiring a conformance review has been performed.

- Batch processing, if allowed, can extend individual transaction process times.

- Recommendations for system, or process enhancements, are rarely implemented in a timely fashion due to the cross-functional nature of most administrative systems, or processes.

- Work in administrative functions is rarely balanced and some functions will operate faster, or slower, than the upstream, or downstream, processes.

- Communication and computer systems can be unreliable.

- The quality and availability of IT support, both internal and external, can cause long transaction processing delays.

- Office machines, critical to transaction processing, can be unreliable, and may be abused or not maintained properly.

- Review and approval requirements are not commensurate with the risk of not performing that activity.

- Approving does not equal reviewing. The administrative Kaizen event and the data gathering necessary to plan Kaizen events are a means of determining if the above listed problems exist, and the frequency of them.

There can be differences between production and administration processes. In the production process, one worker might only perform a single process step, whereas in the administrative process, one worker may perform several steps and be involved in several other processes. Because of this difference, it is important to gather information about the activities of administrative employees before the Kaizen event begins. The data gathered should include everything that happens to an administrative worker over a designated period of time.

- What did the person accomplish?

- What were they supposed to do?

- What happened that prevented them from doing what they were supposed to do?

- Who interfered?

- Why, and at what interval?

- How long should it take to perform a process, or process step?

- How long did it take to perform a process, or process step?

Comparing what was done to what was supposed to have been accomplished will determine if the job description is accurate, or if the work is balanced. Analyzing and categorizing the various reasons why work was interrupted, by whom, and at what interval will provide a hit list for future Kaizen events.

Culture/Value/Technology

The Customer

Technological advancements have had a significant impact on our culture. We have gone from shoppers (on our feet) to browsers (sitting in a chair). As we have grown to accept the positive aspects of these advancements, we have also grown accustomed to the negative aspects, and are essentially letting companies determine value. While these companies may genuinely think that they are providing value options, they may not have anticipated the abuse that could result. For example, in some situations, caller ID technology will almost guarantee that your call will not be answered, and you will be placed into a voice mail system. People used to have to answer the phone when it rang. Now they take a look at the telephone display, and can let your call go to voice mail if they are not in a mood to talk to you. This puts you, and your concerns, in limbo and you are now at the mercy of the person you called; you dare not use your phone, or leave the premises, because that person will be calling you back at any time. (Right?)

Your initial call into most companies will send you off into an elaborate audio menu that is supposed to help direct your call. The best that can happen in this circumstance is that the company actually has a system that works, and you receive immediate gratification. The worst that can happen is that your call is sent to Mr. or Ms. X and they are looking at your name or number on their caller ID display.

We particularly like the recording you get when calling a company that states that your call may be recorded for quality control purposes. We are constantly discussing the miserable experiences we have had trying to resolve problems with these companies but neither of us can remember every getting a return call from the quality person apologizing for the bad treatment or poor service.

Here are some more examples of how the customer is being steered towards value that is based on the cost structure of the service provider.

- Healthcare providers have created low cost health care options (HMO), but you have lost your opportunity to choose the doctor.

- Banks have provided ATM machines for your convenience, but there is a limit to the amount of money you can get. Additionally, you can be charged a fee to get your own money by two different banks, and in most cases the security you had inside the bank is no longer available.

- Insurance companies have created policies that cover every situation that they could be exposed to, yet these policies are impossible to understand, and can not be adequately interpreted by the best of us. When something goes wrong, there is a chance that someone at the insurance company will explain some vague clause that limits liability. A final section in all policies that lists, clearly, everything that is not covered would be helpful. What is it, exactly, that they are afraid of?

The Company

Certain of the technology advances made in the past twenty years were intended to provide businesses with the capability to do more with fewer people. For the most part these IT and communication advancements are excellent tools and can accomplish exactly what their creator's intended.

The problem is that many companies acquired and implemented the technology without doing anything substantial to improve their old processes. The old adage that "computerizing chaos results in computerized chaos" holds true in this situation. If you do not fix the processes that cause customer dissatisfaction when implementing these new technologies, you will have created a totally new problem.

In our experience, a good percentage of companies who acquire new IT and communication technologies do so thinking they are buying a solution. In reality, those technologies are simply tools that should be used in conjunction with efficient processes.

Non-manufacturing companies can improve their processes, and provide their respective services more efficiently, and at a lower cost, by implementing Lean enterprise concepts. We say this with conviction, because a large percentage of the improvements that are made in manufacturing companies relate to the administration areas. We have seen countless Kaizen teams in manufacturing companies assembled to review administrative processes, and they have been very effective. Once these teams have received a brief Lean education covering the elements, rules, and tools of Lean, they have approached the task ahead of them with confidence and have provided Lean solutions to processes that have been in existence for decades.

The aspect of Lean that separates it from most other improvement programs is the participation of all employees in the enterprise. Without the latter, Lean is elusive. Kaizen teams, staffed by cross-functional members, have proven to be a very powerful aspect of Lean. Kaizen teams, staffed with people from all levels and disciplines in the company, is an excellent way to get at the sub-cultures and cross-functional issues that hamper business operations.

8

Lean for Healthcare

Those who say that this cannot be done should go and see others that are doing it…and doing it successfully.
- Brian Furlong and Keith Gilpatrick

"But we are different…" We hear this comment all the time but it is much more prevalent in the healthcare industry. If we had a twenty dollar bill for every time we have heard this comment we could have retired by now. One of the major problems we encounter in the healthcare industry is that it is very inwardly focused. We hear comments like "you must use our terminology" all the time.

There is one manufacturing company we heard about that went to the Emergency Department of a hospital to study what happens when an emergency patient arrives. They took what they learned and applied the same process to machine breakdowns in their factory. What a great idea! We see too few examples of healthcare organizations looking at what happens in other industries. This is one of the primary reasons for Lean being elusive!

So... how different is the healthcare industry?

All organizations - including healthcare organizations - are composed of a series of processes, or sets of actions intended to create value for those who use or depend on them (customers/patients). The more you study all types of organizations the more you realize that, while the end product/service is different, the processes they use to deliver those products/services are remarkably similar. That is why we have yet to come across an industry where Lean principles and concepts cannot be applied.

Let's take a look at some of the similarities between the healthcare industry and all other industries. Each has:

- Processes
- Products and Services
- Equipment must be available and working
- Workplaces must be organized and clean
- Accounting must track and report financial results
- Cultures
- Sub-Cultures
- Customers for similar products and services with different values
- Competition

- Material planning

- Inventory management

- Scheduling - People, Space, Machinery/Equipment

- High Product/Service mix

- Technical training to maintain competitive position

- Waste

- Budgets/Forecasts

- Personnel Issues

- Productivity problems

- Quality Control

- Operating policies and procedures

- Standards/Regulations

- Unilateral decisions that cause havoc with upstream suppliers and downstream customers

- Etc.

Those who say that Lean is not applicable to healthcare, or that treating patients is not the same as making a product, need to focus on the similarities rather than the differences. All industries have thousands of interacting processes and these processes typically contain significant amounts of duplication and waste.

We strongly suggest that healthcare professionals step outside of their own world and go see what others are doing. Look at manufacturing, look at service businesses, look at construction, look at the hospitality industry etc. and then come back and look at those in your own industry who are successfully doing what you may initially think is impossible. We worked with the VP of Quality and Clinical Safety for a large healthcare organization who had visited Toyota and many other companies. While he clearly understood the vast potential for his organization, he spent almost a year persuading others in his organization to support a Lean initiative.

Who is interested?

Every industry we encounter is anxious to see what the healthcare industry is going to do about their year-on-year staggering cost increases. These costs are negatively impacting competitiveness in all industries and forcing some companies to move overseas to countries where wages and benefits are not such a burden. Domestically, many companies/organizations (including healthcare organizations) are cutting back on their healthcare benefits. Coverage is being reduced, deductibles are being increased and some companies are beginning to opt for savings accounts as opposed to healthcare coverage. We hear and read about patients who now find it less expensive to fly to another country to have a medical procedure than to have it performed in the United States (in other industries we would call this outsourcing).

As organizations cut back on healthcare benefits and individuals get more autonomy in terms of how they spend the healthcare dollars, efficient and cost effective organizations will thrive. Others will simply cease to exist. (We know of one hospital which is about to close its doors because its costs greatly exceed its revenues and this has been the case for some time. Management at this hospital dismissed Lean as being irrelevant.)

It is probably fair to say that the healthcare industry in general is urgently in need of Lean treatment.

We need to point out that we are most impressed by the genuine caring and compassionate attitude for patients we have seen in almost every healthcare professional we have met. As we discuss Lean for Healthcare we are not addressing the clinical aspects of care (although implementing Lean will benefit those aspects as well). That is best left to the qualified doctors, nurses and other professionals who do an outstanding job. We are addressing the processes used to deliver patient care and other services. Like most other industries, these processes contain large amounts of waste.

Waste

In healthcare, as in other industries, there are eight different types of waste. Please review our earlier section on waste. There are many regulatory processes in place that cannot be changed right now (non value added but required). Other processes revolve around Medicare and insurance claims and while these may seem to be untouchable at this point that does not mean that improvements cannot be made. All remaining processes should be reviewed so that waste can be identified and eliminated.

Lean Elements

Each of the five Lean elements of Value, Value Stream, Flow, Pull and Perfection apply in healthcare as they do in any other business. When we talk about value we mean patient or customer value. In many healthcare organizations the term customer is used to refer to physicians but don't forget that everyone has an internal customer also.

When you look at the value stream you should consider everything has happens from admittance to discharge or other major processes that have a logical starting and finishing point.

Flow is key! What interrupts Flow? Where does the process stop? Look for complexity – the more complicated the process the more likely it is that Flow will be interrupted. Can you make the process simple? Remember, simple is the target but simple is anything but easy. One OR nurse told us that her philosophy was "touch it only once." We should use that mantra across all processes in all businesses.

When you are looking at the Pull element of Lean, consider any operation where work is pushed to the next downstream step whether that step is ready for it or not. To create effective Flow work should only be moved to the next step when the need has been signaled. Otherwise, it will sit there until someone is available to work on it. When that happens Flow has stopped. Key Lean tools that are critical to Flow and Pull are Work Balancing and Level Loading. Do everything you can to balance the work and level the load. It may not be possible everywhere but that does not mean we should not attempt to do so.

When pursuing the Perfection element ask yourself the question "Am I better today than I was yesterday." Let that guide you. Apply the same energy and attitude that is applied to the clinical aspects of healthcare.

Lean Rules

All four Lean Rules are applicable to healthcare. Standard Work will help to eliminate variation in the process which in turn will help to eliminate quality problems. You must have the desire, the will and the tenacity to implement Standard Work. This is not easy and it is not glitzy. Once you have Standard Work in place, you must enforce the necessary disciplines to ensure that it is followed. One of the lessons learned from organizations that have been on a Lean journey for some time is that they wished they had paid more attention to this subject. *Without Standard work Lean will be elusive!*

Limit people and material movement. These two rules are certainly applicable in healthcare. In large (and even small) facilities, look at the distances that nurses, doctors, supplies, lab samples, food service etc. travel every day. Obviously facility layout is an issue and you are not likely to be able to change that unless you are currently constructing a new facility. Do everything possible to bring supplies to the point of use. Utilize C.O.W.S (computers on wheels) instead of multiple trips back and forth to record or get data. Fully understand why people have to leave their work areas and relentlessly pursue other alternatives. While people are walking, searching, transporting, retrieving etc. they are generating Waste.

By now you have probably gotten the message that we are passionate about the Education rule of Lean. Doctors, Nurses, Pharmacists, Technicians, IT personnel, Purchasing personnel, Food Service personnel etc. should all receive a Lean Education. Then use the power of cross-functionality to your advantage. We were told by one person that you will not likely get a physician to participate in a Kaizen event and another immediately followed with an example of a doctor working with a saw and hammer in the Emergency Department at 2.00 a.m. to improve the layout of that area. People will not likely participate in Lean improvements unless they fully understand what Lean is about. For example, our Lean

269

for Healthcare web-based training program in being used by one Home Healthcare organization as a way to accomplish this for people with limited time availability and conflicting schedules. When you say it can't be done, please remember that others are doing it. Without a comprehensive education Lean is elusive!

Lean Tools

Most of the Lean tools are applicable to healthcare. Even seemingly unrelated tools such as Total Productive Maintenance (TPM) and Quick Change Over are important. In one hospital, a nurse made the comment "TPM is critical – lives depend on our equipment being in perfect working order." Quick Change can be directly applied to the changeover of patients in the Operating Room, Emergency Department or to maximize bed occupancy. Mistake-proofing is one Lean tool that should be applied universally. We heard of one case where a patient was not asked if he had any hearing aids before an MRI. The damage to his hearing aids cost the hospital five thousand dollars. We strongly suggest that every corrective action form include a section on how mistake-proofing has been utilized to prevent the error from occurring again.

Value Stream Mapping, Process Mapping, 6S, Kanban, Work Balancing, Level Loading, One Need Flow, DFEU, 5 Why's, Spaghetti Charts, Takt Time and Visual Workplace all have applications in healthcare organizations. Can you apply every tool in every circumstance? No! But apply them wherever you can and don't let anyone tell you that they are not applicable in your industry. Instead of saying they don't apply, ask the question "how can I apply them?" Don't allow Lean to be elusive because you can't get past the mindset that these tools are for manufacturing companies only. They are not!

Productivity

Like other industries, healthcare organizations have attempted to implement improvement programs that pressure operating personnel to be productive and they measure productivity on a daily, weekly, or monthly basis.

At one large healthcare organization where we were conducting Lean facilitator training, we found that some employees were sent home without pay on occasions when bed occupancy was not at targeted levels. We were also told by the students that participation in Kaizen events would be difficult as no allowance was made for this in their productivity goals. So, while the training was approved, there was no formal approval for the follow-up activities. It was our understanding that senior management did not really understand the commitment required when implementing Lean.

A note of caution: if employees believe that they will be sent home or laid-off as a result of improving processes, they are highly unlikely to help you to improve them. They may well correlate being sent home as in the circumstance outlined above to being sent home when less work is required as a result of waste elimination.

When all you focus on is productivity as a metric, Lean could be elusive. When you focus on eliminating waste, productivity will be the result.

Concrete Heads

One of our clients uses the acronym C.A.V.E. (Citizens Against Virtually Everything) people to describe concrete heads. Healthcare has its share of these people just like any other industry. On one occasion during an orientation session at one major hospital we were interviewing the Director of Pharmacy. For one full hour, he went out of his way to point out to us how little we knew about his business and did everything possible to demean our knowledge and possible contribution to his operation. He had zero interest in any system that might be an alternative to the way he operated his department.

In healthcare, when you are applying concepts that originated in manufacturing you are likely to encounter a number of people who think like this. If we cannot change this attitude then Lean will be elusive. We need to give people every possible opportunity to participate but when all avenues have been exhausted and they will not change they must be removed.

Summary

There are many healthcare organizations that describe themselves as non-profit. Unfortunately, we have seen more situations than we would like to where that is a mindset as opposed to a legal entity. When people believe that you don't have to make a profit then it will be very difficult to get them to identify and eliminate Waste in the process. Healthcare organizations are businesses like any other and they must make a profit to survive. Whether you call it profit or margin is irrelevant. Typically margins are very small in healthcare and it does not take a lot to go wrong for this to be a major problem.

Instead of using the phrase "I'll believe it when I see it" perhaps you should consider the phrase "I'll see it when I believe it." There is way too much evidence out there to support the fact that Lean works in all industries; including healthcare. Your strategy has to begin with a belief that Lean can bring about amazing benefits for patients, customers, employees and suppliers. If you see it as a journey rather than a project and you are not obsessed by instant gratification then you can put a long-term strategy together that can totally transform your organization.

Healthcare is changing and healthcare organizations must change also. Remember, if you do what you've always done – you will get what you always got. Look at the examples of healthcare organizations that have embraced Lean, learn from them and then apply it in your own organization. What have you got to loose?

CHAPTER
9

Lean People

It's never crowded along the extra mile.
- Dr. Wayne Dyer

An enterprise is a collection of people working together to produce a product or service. To have a Lean Enterprise, you need Lean-thinking people. Think about where you work. Now think about where you work without any people in it. It is simply buildings, equipment and materials. People make the enterprise either successful or unsuccessful.

We discussed change earlier in this book and talked about the process of change. One of the main reasons that people resist change is because what they do works. It may not work the way you would like it to, but it works nonetheless. In a Lean Enterprise, people must be willing to view the system from a value stream perspective rather than a departmental perspective. They must understand that the system is a whole made up of the sum of all the parts and they way all the parts work together determines how well the system as a whole works. Ask a manager if she/he would be willing to give up part of their budget or a couple of people to benefit another department and see what kind of response you get. One of the key challenges facing many organizations as they implement Lean is the silo mentality. *When the silo mentality prevails, Lean is elusive!*

There are several traits that Lean people ideally should have – especially those who champion or lead the process. These are:

- Customer-focused

- Enterprise-wide thinker

- Adaptive

- Initiative

- Innovative

- Team player

- Center of influence

- Sense of urgency

- Tenacity

- Great listener

- Good sense of humor

To be successful with Lean, the vast majority of people must be on-board. While this will not happen immediately, it should happen over time. When Lean leaders display the characteristics outlined above, others will be more willing to participate.

Lean and the 7 Habits

One of the most successful books ever written is *The 7 Habits of Highly Effective People* by Dr. Stephen R. Covey (published by Simon & Schuster 1989) We strongly recommend this book which has sold over 15 million copies. As a Lean Enterprise requires highly effective people, let's take a very brief look at how the 7 Habits align with Lean.

Habit 1: Be Proactive

Lean requires a proactive mindset. We must take responsibility for the situation that exists today (after all, we created it) and for the one that we wish to create for the future. Behaviors must change and we must understand that existing behaviors are a product of our own conscious choices. Proactive people make value-based choices. It is not what happens to us that is important but how we respond to what happens to us.

Little will change in an enterprise as you move towards Lean unless behaviors change. We must understand what causes current behaviors and remove those causes. Lean is very much a Go See, Go Do process. Being proactive is a must.

Habit 2: Begin with the End in Mind

Imagine you are already there. Visualize what the organization will look like in the future, how it will operate, what the mindset of the people will be, how you will respond to customers, how profitable and successful you will be and so on. Think from the end – all the while understanding that you have a long way to go. Create and communicate the vision and then create the passion to achieve that vision. In other words, lead! Do not tell people what to do or how to do it! Instead, make them part of the vision, employ their creativity and enlist their help to achieve the desired end results. Along the way, ensure you are doing what is needed to facilitate their success. It is critical that they feel that they are an important part of the process and the key to future success.

Habit 3: Put First Things First

Look at how people currently spend their time. How many people in your organization are working on what is important? They may be working on what is apparently urgent, but that does not mean it is important. For example, when the tele-phone rings, we typically regard that as urgent. However, it may not be important. Study the time management quadrant created by Dr. Covey and see where the majority of people's time is spent in your organization. Is it spent on tasks that are?

- Important and urgent

- Important but not urgent

- Not important and urgent

- Not important and not urgent.

One of the most frequent obstacles we encounter as organizations start the Lean journey is that people tell us "we have no time to do this – we are very busy right now." There is never a time when they are not busy. We must understand that we have all the time there is and there is nothing we can do to create any more time. What happened even one second ago is over and we cannot recover it. The key question we have to ask is "how are the people in our organization spending their time today?"

We find that most managers and other associates spend the majority of their time on minor crises, hand-off's and logistical complexity. When you map the Value Stream or the process you will see just how much time is spent on waste – definitely not urgent and not important. In some cases, we even have people employed full time in positions that could be regarded as waste. We frequently encounter situations where people are not allowed to participate in Kaizen events (important) and we subsequently find that they are busy dealing with something that is neither urgent nor important.

Obviously, we regard Lean as being both urgent and important. Who is working on it in your organization? Are you working on it proactively, or are you paying it lip service because you are working on activities that are not important and not urgent? As you examine these questions you may be very surprised by the answers you uncover.

Habit 4: Think Win/Win

In a Lean Enterprise everybody wins (except, perhaps, the competition)! Customers win because they receive better value. Employees win because they are more involved, the work they do is important and they grow both personally and professionally. Suppliers win because they become a true partner. The organization as a whole wins because Lean helps to secure a long-term profitable future.

We need to be reminded from time-to-time that win/win is a philosophy not a technique. We are so used to thinking that if we win then someone else has to loose. That is very much the authoritarian approach and one we encounter all the time. If you want success in a Lean environment, everyone should win.

Habit 5: Seek First to Understand, Then to be Understood

How much time have you spent in your life developing the skill of listening? Do you prescribe before you diagnose? Do you try to enforce your solution on a problem you don't even understand because you are looking at the symptoms not the cause; or because you are reacting to perception as opposed to reality? Have you encountered people who are in a conversation waiting for their turn to talk who frequently say things that suggest that they were not listening? People with this trait are committed only to their own thoughts.

We often encounter people who spend lots of time solving the wrong problem or a problem that doesn't even exist.

Knowing how to be understood is also critical to the previous habit which is win/win. As a participant in a Kaizen event, it is very important that you take the time to ensure that you understand the problem (first understand) and that you explain your proposed solutions or ideas (then be understood).

Habit 6: Synergize

Is everyone in your organization on the same page or even the same chapter? Are the people in your organization doing what is best for them as opposed to what's best for the organization as a whole? Does everyone understand the vision; support it and then work together towards the achievement of the goals that support that vision?

If the Lean initiative is just a seemingly incompatible series of time-consuming projects that lack direction, it will be elusive! Everyone needs to be on board and pulling in the same direction. Policy Deployment will help to accomplish that but you must also be willing to create a level of excitement to go with it. Communicate, then communicate, then communicate; unceasingly! In parallel, establish a recognition system that rewards synergistic behavior.

Habit 7: Sharpen the Saw

In a Lean Enterprise, you help to ensure success when you give people workable tools to solve problems. If the saw is not sharp, it will take significantly longer to fell the tree. Many organizations we encounter are far too busy felling to take time for sharpening.

Providing everyone in your organization with a Lean education (the fourth rule) is sharpening the saw. When you have done this, you have a lot more people who are capable of felling the tree. This habit is required for all of the other habits and integral to success with Lean. **Without it, Lean will be elusive!**

Lean Thinkers

Over time, you must get more and more people to become Lean thinkers. Couple that with the inherent creativity that is in all of us and you will have a lifetime business philosophy and formula for continued success. How could it not be?

10

Rumor Control

**A secret is diluted by the square of the number
of those who have heard it.**
- *Robert Half*

The one thing that every company attempting a Lean
conversion will experience is the problem of Rumor
Control. If education and policy deployment are not at
the top of the implementation list, rumors will circulate, and
the success of the transformation could be negatively impacted. Bad news always travels faster, and to more places,
than good news. It will take only one person to spread the bad
news and an army of managers to correct the misconceptions.
A combination of education and Policy Deployment will get
you off on the right foot.

Having introduced Rumor Control as an issue, we need to discuss Policy Deployment and the Human Resource issues associated with a Lean implementation.

It is inevitable that management will want to attack the low hanging fruit that is available when implementing certain Lean concepts. Establishing the Flow and Pull elements of Lean can have an impact on direct labor costs. By balancing production and producing at Takt Time, often, processes are combined, and fewer people are needed to produce the same or a greater amount than the old process. The way you handle this situation is very important.

In considering headcount reductions, we should look at two different scenarios.

1) You are implementing Lean because you will go out of business otherwise.

In this situation, you are probably experiencing an attrition rate that is higher than normal, because employees see the writing on the wall, and are leaving your company as soon as they can find employment elsewhere. Alternatively, employees see the loss of their jobs as inevitable, and are waiting for the hammer to fall.

In this scenario, a company can introduce Lean as a program to stem the flow; improve financial performance; get product quality, cost and margins under control; improve service levels; and secure jobs that are in danger or restore jobs that have been lost. While this is not the best of situations for a Lean transformation, it can cause fewer problems if employees believe that management is doing the right thing.

2) You are implementing Lean because you want to be ahead of the curve, and be the supplier of choice for every possible customer of your products.

While this is the best reason to go Lean, it can cause more problems with the implementation if the program is not introduced properly, and the subject of headcount reductions has not been resolved and addressed directly as part of the introduction and education phase. While the headcount reduction rate could be higher than the normal attrition rate, a good philosophy to follow, if it is possible, is that the company will not release people whose jobs have become redundant, but will do everything possible to avoid hiring to fill positions vacated through attrition. Instead, the company would prioritize cross-training and moving employees to other positions.

Because Lean is implemented via Kaizen events that are staffed with employees from all areas of your company, it is difficult for these people to participate in a program that will eliminate jobs held by their friends or peers.

Management must make the difficult decisions early in the planning phase and communicate quickly, and honestly, to all employees. If you are not consistent in this aspect of your Lean transformation you will experience great difficulty.

The Policy Deployment aspect of the Lean transformation is just a critical as the human resource issues. You must create policies that are consistent with Lean concepts. You cannot adopt certain aspects of Lean and ignore others. When you are considering the value aspect of your business processes, you must be consistent throughout all processes. If there is no value associated with a process, or process step, it must be eliminated. To eliminate some, but not all, non-value-added processes or process steps, will send a very confusing or negative message to those attempting to create change in your company.

A review of current policies and procedures is recommended as part of the planning process. Policies and procedures that are suspect should become the subject of specific Kaizen events, with the objective of providing the control required while eliminating the obvious waste.

Concrete heads love to spread rumors, and their primary targets are those individuals in the company who are more likely to be impacted by the anticipated changes and who can influence the success of the program. Don't give these concrete heads the ammunition that they seek to destroy your implementation program.

A good example is the typical authorization matrix. These matrices have grown over the years to become operational roadblocks. They were developed to provide controls that were easier to implement than a process that provided the same control, but did not require the same scrutiny. It is only in rare instances that a manager's approval adds value to the process, yet the need for that approval can bring the process to a halt. We are not suggesting that a company eliminate prudent or fiscal controls; we are suggesting that those controls can be maintained by developing processes that are efficient and realistic with regard to risk exposure and cost. Concrete heads love to seek out the individuals who may lose some of their authority, and get the negative juices flowing.

A practical example of this is a specific Kaizen that was reviewing the Engineering Change Order (ECO) process of a manufacturer of small motors. The analysis of three years of ECO's indicated that the average time to process an ECO in the company was eighty-three days. The value-added time involved in the ECO process was approximately 13 hours. The difference between the 83 days and the 13 hours was the time it took an ECO to travel around the engineering and manufacturing operations getting the appropriate authorization signatures. When a manager, who needed to authorize the change or an aspect of the work involved in the change, was not available, the paperwork associated with the change did not move until the signature was received. In this case, there were over a dozen signatures required in the original process. After the Kaizen event, the number of required signatures was reduced to three and in each case there was a time limit established for the approval. An escalation process was put in place if the signature was not obtained within that time limit. As the Lean facilitators for this event, we were called into the office of the general manager on a number of occasions because he had heard rumors about our plans to eliminate certain levels of approval. This will be a common occurrence early in your Lean transformation, and the best you can do as a Lean facilitator is to caution your Kaizen team about discussing the interim phases of the event.

Lean corporate goals and metrics for measuring performance also need to be addressed as part of the Policy Deployment aspect of the Lean transformation plan. These should be communicated to all employees. An example of this would be to opt for measuring performance to customer demand, as opposed to traditional productivity or machine utilization metrics.

A word of caution

Before we continue we must add that if you are attempting, or contemplating, a Lean Enterprise transformation, there is only one Lean Enterprise concept. That is the one advocated by James P. Womack and Daniel T. Jones. Many consultants or business process improvement specialists have taken selected aspects of Lean and attempted to package them as the solution to your business process problems. Taken as separate facets of Lean, no one piece will bring the success you will receive from the whole. You are either going Lean following the Lean concepts presented by Womack and Jones, or you are attempting something else, and we wish you luck.

As you locate and hire employees with prior Lean experience the nature of your Lean program becomes more important. If you are attempting to implement something other than the true Lean Enterprise concepts the new employees will add to the rumor control problem once they realize that you are attempting something else. A good policy to adopt with regard to rumor control is to formally publish all rumors and provide a response to each. Another rumor control device is to have every meeting in the company begin with the question "So what have you heard about Lean recently"?

Failing to control the rumor mill will contribute to the elusiveness of Lean.

11

Educate

If you think education is expensive, have you checked the cost of ignorance lately?
- Unknown

Early in our attempts to create an E-learning, Lean Enterprise training program we visited a major U.S. corporation to discuss the prospects of having that corporation use our initial version of what is now marketed as "Lean Mastery". We knew we were doomed when the executive in charge of the Lean transformation at the company stated that he thought James Womack was a great historian and went on to outline his vision of a Lean implementation program. This company did not believe that everyone in the organization should participate in the Lean transformation. The "vision" at this company was that a select few, highly educated individuals, would be trained and operate as project teams to implement Lean.

If you consider Womack an historian, you have not kept current with everything he has done since he published Lean Thinking. We subscribe to his newsletter and communicate with his organization frequently. Womack is constantly exploring the success, or lack thereof, of Lean Enterprise transformations. In recent times, his newsletters have focused on important issues such as educating everyone, standard work, value stream mapping, and cautioning those contemplating offshore moves or partnerships to do Lean Math.

We like to think that those of us who are Lean Thinkers are open-minded and have no fear of the exchange of knowledge and best practices. We chose not to argue the Womack historian comment or the Lean implementation vision described, and moved on. In the three years since that meeting, we believe we have a greater understanding of Lean and are effective Lean consultants because we have stuck to our convictions that there is only one Lean Enterprise concept, and that everyone in the enterprise should be educated and involved in the implementation program. Consultants are useful in introducing Lean and providing initial Lean facilitator training, or training aids, but try to get them out of the process as fast as you can. For sure, they can implement Lean but your organization will have more Lean Thinkers, and be able to sustain the momentum of the program, if you assume the responsibility of educating everyone and implementing Lean in your company.

The most critical aspect of the Lean Enterprise implementation is education. Executives need an extensive Lean education to competently select Lean as the solution; establish a Lean organization structure; and properly plan the implementation. Lower tier managers, supervisors, and other employees need a Lean education to enhance their ability to understand the concepts, and participate in the radical changes that need to take place in all of your business processes. Suppliers and customers need the education as well. Suppliers need to be aware of your motivation, and strategy, for changing your relationship with them. Your customers need to understand that you are enhancing the quality of your products, and your ability to meet their requirements for delivery, while reducing their investment in inventory as well as their total cost of product. We believe that educating everyone in the company as soon as possible will reduce the impact of rumors, reduce the total time for the Lean conversion and will move critical cost reductions closer to your start date. Consider the human element. If only a select few are chosen to implement Lean, the remaining employees will inevitably find a way to rebel, and this could sabotage your attempts to create the changes necessary to become a Lean operation. In our experience, there is no one class of employee that operates better than another in a Lean transformation. If anything, non-management employees are more likely to recognize and understand that the current system is broken. It is not uncommon for executive management to have lost touch with the way the system works. They are often surprised when current system capabilities are presented along with recommendations for improvement It is our experience that the primary reason for slow progress or unsuccessful Lean transformations is the lack of education. It seems that the majority within corporate management is so busy managing the chaos that exists in their operations that they are not inclined, or cannot afford the time, to get a good Lean education. As we stated earlier in this book, it is rare that we get the opportunity to train at the highest level in an organization. It is not for the lack of promoting the need. Every piece of literature that we produce emphatically states that the first group of people needing a Lean education is the executives. We are frequently asked to speak at breakfast or dinner meetings and we take this opportunity to emphasize the need for executive education prior to the implementation of Lean.

It is not uncommon that on the opening day of a training session we are informed that executive so-an-so will not be attending, as planned, because he or she could not get away from his or her operation for a few days. The substitute for the executive usually has no clue why he or she is at the training session, and rarely has the same level of authority and responsibility as the planned attendee.

It is also not uncommon that people scheduled for Kaizen events fail to show up because their managers cannot afford to have them absent from their work. With one client, we adopted a program called "Out Sick". We would visit the manager who had kept an employee from a Kaizen event, and we would ask that manager what he or she would do if the person involved had called in sick? The usual, and obvious, response was that they would have gotten along somehow. We then announced that that individual had called in sick and the manager would have to get along somehow. This worked well and was only needed for a short period of time. The executive who hired us to institutionalize Lean supported this strategy, and would not entertain any discussion regarding the availability of employees to participate in Kaizen events. Participating in a Lean transformation is not an option. Participating in a Lean transformation cannot be accomplished without first receiving an intensive Lean education. Trust us, if you are the chief operating officer, you will not experience any satisfactory level of success if you do not educate yourself and insist that everyone in your company be educated. So create your own "Out Sick" program and make sure that you, and your direct reports, are "out sick" for four days while receiving a Lean treatment prior to implementation.

It is OK to hire a Lean expert or consultant to guide you through a Lean transformation. But that employee or consultant should not be the primary vehicle for implementing Lean in your organization. Your Lean expert should have educating every employee a part of his or her Lean vision. Once again, as the chief executive, the responsibility for the implementation of Lean is yours. If your strategy is to delegate that responsibility, it will get delegated again and again until the program has no real impact or relevance. By the way, if you are serious about implementing a new corporate culture, how could you be busy doing things the old way and expect anyone in your company to believe that you want to embrace change?

The executive education should be intensive and cover all aspects of Lean and a Lean transformation plan. Executives need to argue or discuss the concepts, and believe that Lean will produce results. Executives need to be viewed as the experts in Lean concepts. How could any employee in your company think you were serious about changing the company culture if you are not aware of the elements, rules, and tools of Lean? By the way, it is also expected that the executives will demonstrate their commitment by being present at Kaizen presentations, and challenge the teams to be more aggressive and creative in their Lean projects.

We know of an executive who had been put out to pasture, and was assigned the responsibility of managing a large distribution center. This executive was later told he had to attend Lean training, and he went to that training session kicking and biting because he saw this as a bother, and he did not have the desire to participate in another improvement program. He had accepted his position at the company, and just wanted to wait out the time until his retirement. When he returned from the training session he had become a new man. He had become a new manager. He sent all of his direct reports to similar training sessions and turned his distribution center into an outstanding Lean operation. He did not stop there. He became so vocal in his support for Lean that he was given assignments outside of his distribution center operation, and eventually his status in the company changed significantly. The transition this man made was truly miraculous. He went from sitting in his office with the door closed, to traveling around the globe educating and implementing Lean. His success in helping other divisions on a voluntary basis put his name back on the corporate radar.

We believe there is a substantial population within the business community that has grown discouraged by the status quo attitude of management. They have become casualties of the corporate political environment, and have reverted to tactics similar to those of the distribution center manager, and are just trying to exist. Embracing Lean concepts will help these people to become re-energized. While some might look to the current pool of executives to manage a Lean transformation, we would suggest that you train everybody and see who emerges as a real agent of change.

On a similar note, it is very discouraging for us to see that the desire of those who want change is rarely matched by those who have the responsibility for change. The main reason for this is the territorialism that is prevalent in almost all businesses. As Lean consultants, we wrestle with this territorial issue on a daily basis. We struggle constantly with our own client base to get everybody educated and on board. Even with our record of success at individual plants, we see management that still has the tendency to resist change will do so until the hammer is dropped on them. It is almost as though the risk of resisting change is less of a threat to them than the thought of letting go of their traditional management theories and their territorial control.

After your executive team has been educated and believes and demonstrates that Lean is not optional, the next thing they should learn is that you expect them to work as a team. The chief executive, should develop little tolerance for territorial issues and confront those who demonstrate any such propensity.

Once you have educated yourself and your direct reports, you should begin planning your Lean transformation. Again, one of the more critical aspects of your Lean transformation plan will be education. You will need a cadre of Lean facilitators who will be responsible for Lean education and initial Kaizen activity. Traditional classroom training techniques are almost a necessity for your Lean cadre, but do not wait for these people to get trained, and engaged, in your Lean implementation before others in your company have the opportunity to learn about Lean. We recommend that you provide the entire population with an opportunity to learn Lean concepts.

We have worked for several years to develop a solution to the problem of educating everyone in the organization. This product is called Lean Mastery ™ - a unique, low cost, interactive, education and implementation toolbox designed to be deployed across the Internet, an intranet or on a network, so that it is readily available to all employees. The payback is rapid when Lean Mastery is used in combination with an aggressive education and implementation plan. It is recommended that employees complete projects so that the education is put into practice. Lean Mastery facilitates all learning styles, namely, read, hear teach, do and write. The software utilizes visual, audio, interactive and classroom tools to provide the best possible learning experience. A case study is provided that follows the implementation of Lean. Lean Mastery provides access to power point presentations that are designed for classroom use. It includes all of the forms used in a Lean implementation. Many of these are interactive, and automatically generate charts etc. that can be used in management presentations. Lean Mastery conforms to all the e-learning industry standards. A test module that randomly selects questions is also available, and reports test results electronically to both the student and to a specified training person in your company. Lean Mastery can also be customized to include your company specific logos, data and forms etc.

Whatever your means of education, be sure to get Lean in some form out into your company as fast as possible. We have documented evidence that an early education, offered to everyone in a company, can speed up the implementation and provide a significantly higher rate of success. *Without a comprehensive education program a highly successful Lean Enterprise is elusive.*

Another vital aspect of the Education phase of the Lean transformation is whatever type or combination of types of education are selected you would be wise to require a Lean project utilizing the concepts learned before giving credit for that education. We use this technique as part of our consulting and continuing education programs. Every individual we train is required to conduct a Kaizen event during or shortly after that training. If you do not adopt a similar program you will not gain the momentum that you will need to sustain the continuous improvement program. ***It is estimated that people forget 70% of what they learn if it is not put into practice in 72 hours.***

We can tell you that almost every facilitator we have trained has been somewhat intimidated by the magnitude of the change associated with Lean. The strategy of requiring a Kaizen event during or after the training will give facilitators the confidence they need to become active in your Lean transformation.

CHAPTER

12

Planning

By failing to prepare you are preparing to fail
- Benjamin Franklin

T he most disturbing aspect of our experience in the
consulting business is that, in many cases, companies
that we have dealt with have been found wanting with
regard to a Lean plan. Poor planning, or the lack of any plan,
has been apparent during our sales discussions or by listening
to people who attend our training sessions or seminars. We are
constantly confronted by students who are the first in their
companies to get a Lean education, and very few of them are
at the executive level. These people come to our classes and,
without exception, leave with an appreciation for Lean and a
"let's go" attitude. What happens to these students when they
return to their respective companies is a mystery to us. What
we do know is that each of those students had to complete a
Kaizen project as part of our training and, again without

exception, presented results that were very impressive. To be fair, we have encountered good Lean people in some of these companies. The problem is that management assigns the responsibility for implementing Lean to these people, as they have done with other improvement programs, and then assumes that one person, or a small team of people, will be successful. Lean requires a culture change. The most significant culture change is that executive management must be engaged in the implementation of Lean, and never relinquish the responsibility to anyone else. Every executive in the company must be a "Lean Thinker", and everything done from the point in which the program commences must address specific Lean goals using recognized Elements, Rules, and Tools of Lean Enterprise. This is where many of the companies we have dealt with have faltered.

If you are a CEO and want to assign the responsibility for the implementation to someone in your company; make sure this person reports directly to you and has a very strong mandate for the task ahead.

Caution!

If you are contemplating hiring a "Lean Expert", be thorough in your search. Lean knowledge alone will not ensure success. Candidates should be expected to detail how they will organize and facilitate the Lean implementation. If you are the CEO, keep in mind that you are looking for someone to assist in the planning and to facilitate the implementation. The responsibility for the implementation is yours.

Do not attempt to plan a Lean Enterprise implementation until every executive and key lower tier manager has received a Lean education. The first phase of your plan should be to have your Lean expert (or someone from the outside) provide this Lean training. Avoid planning prior to adopting top tier policies, goals, and metrics that are based on a solid Lean foundation. A few weeks spent on the education, policy deployment, and planning phases will provide a handsome payback, and the timeline for the implementation will be shortened. As we have stated numerous times throughout this book, there is an abundance of evidence to prove that poorly educated management and poorly conceived implementation plans do not deliver the desired results.

The second most critical aspect of your Lean planning is the Value Stream Mapping phase. Each major product group should have a value stream map. You must determine what value is for each product group, and reflect how your current processes deliver that value. A good value stream map should provide the roadmap for your improvement plan. In this phase, your Lean education is critical. You will not recognize the opportunity for improvement in your current value stream if you look at the results from the traditional mass manufacturing viewpoint. Do not ignore this phase of planning. When you are looking for your Lean expert, be sure that Value Stream Mapping is a part of his or her Lean approach.

Be aggressive with goals and timelines. One aspect of the cultural change must be to schedule and conduct improvement activities. Avoid traditional behavior that often results in stagnation because participants with political, or territorial, issues make it impossible to get beyond the planning and discussion phase.

Lean activity must be the number one priority. The one problem we guarantee you will have is how to break free of the current chaos in your company. The people in your organization who are fighting the daily fires will have a difficult time dealing with the transition. Somehow they need to keep a finger in the dyke and participate in the improvement program simultaneously. Be patient, as difficult as this phase of the implementation is, at some point the tide will change and your organization will eventually be spending more time on the improvement activities.

Early in the transition phase, you must confront those individuals in your company who are reluctant to, or refuse to change. Once employees at any level in your organization have received Lean training and have been made aware of your Lean goals, they must participate in the change process. A reluctance to change is very different from a refusal to change. People who are reluctant to change need to be assured that the company is committed, and that their participation is valued.

The person who refuses to participate is a "Concrete Head". You must address the "Concrete Head" issue early by creating a strong human resource policy that addresses employees who do not support the program. Concrete Heads must be eliminated as soon as possible; their presence in your company can have a very detrimental effect on a smooth Lean transition.

It is very important that you are not functionally selective in your Lean implementation. Your focus should be the entire enterprise. Prepare a chart that presents every activity in your company, and ensure that each aspect of your business operation is exposed to Lean. Also, include suppliers and customers in your Lean activities wherever possible.

Do not look for a magic sequence for implementing Lean. Your plan should simply include all aspects of your business and results should be expected from each. It has been our experience that manufacturing is the traditional first target for the Lean initiative. While this strategy gets to the low hanging fruit, and can provide a showcase for Lean, we suggest that you dispel the manufacturing only focus quickly. There are several reasons for this.

- If your focus remains in manufacturing Lean will be viewed as a manufacturing program.

- People with the talent and energy for creating change may be in functions that are outside the manufacturing loop.

- You need to establish cross-functional cooperation early in your implementation program.

- Administrative Kaizen events can have significant
  impacts on your manufacturing value stream.

- You need to get to every aspect of your Value
  Stream Map early in your implementation.

As we stated earlier, few plans survive initial contact. A review of your Lean plan should become a part of every executive meeting. No executive should be excluded from this review. React quickly and decisively when you notice stagnation, or a reluctance to act upon the plan.

While we have said there is no magic sequence for implementing Lean we believe, as other experts do, that the best place to start is 5S. The 5S program provides great visual impact for everyone in your company, and will signal major change. 5S will also challenge your commitment to Lean and the culture change. If implementing 5S requires a lot of work, and the before and after visual is astounding (as it usually is), you may still experience great difficulty in maintaining the new look. The before 5S look reflected the real culture that existed, and you will have to be on your toes to maintain the after 5S look. If you let the 5S program slip just a little bit, the message received by everyone will be that you are not committed to a culture change.

Remember that it is very important that you keep the Rules of Lean in mind as you plan and implement Lean. When you change, or create a new process, employ standard work; every attempt should be made to limit travel of material and people through your processes; get everyone in your company involved by training to the lowest level in the organization.

Let's review some issues that may be inherent in your existing corporate culture. As agents of change, we are constantly confronted with the sub-cultures that exist in most organizations. In addition to the subcultures we also run into the differences between the formal and informal processes. While the existence of sub-cultures and formal vs. informal systems is probably no surprise to our readers, the existence of both can cause problems when you are attempting to implement Lean. If, in your own mind, you manage to perform a candid and effective evaluation of your current systems during the value stream mapping process, you may get a few surprises when you attempt to make changes because the sub-cultures and informal processes start to appear. You may encounter statements like these.

- "Oh we haven't followed that policy in years"

- "Our manager told us years ago to ignore that process step"

- "We have not updated that rate schedule"

- "No one ever told me about that policy"

- "Yeah, we knew about that policy but we told everybody it was not workable, and no one listened".

We have heard just about everything imaginable as to why the informal processes have developed. Limiting participation in your Lean transformation will make detecting the informal systems a costly venture.

You will be sent off on a lot of wild goose chases before you get to the real process flow. Do not be surprised if you find that there are informal processes in your organization. For the most part the existence of these is an indication that prior programs, or management philosophies were not effective, and your people had to find workable alternatives to get their jobs done. Working with the people that created these informal systems, and showing real interest in providing workable solutions, is much more effective, and the changes made will likely be sustainable. The sub-culture is sometimes more difficult to detect, but no less significant. Here are some examples.

- Safety procedures could be ignored by groups of workers, and this becomes the standard for anyone joining those groups.

- Theft on a small scale, but at a high frequency might be known, and tolerated, by certain individuals because they feel there is a tradeoff between allowing minor theft and getting people to perform.

- Individuals at lower levels in your organization can have a big following at their peer level, and will decide which rules and procedures they, and the group, will follow.

- The influence executives can have in their respective organizations can have a significant impact on the effectiveness of corporate mandates. Once they apply their interpretation of the mandate and it gets passed down through their organizations, the end result can be quite different from the original intention.

- Machines and entire processes can be damaged because someone wants to express their displeasure about some aspect of the current culture.

- Recommendations for process improvements are sometimes stifled without good reason.

The latter issue of stifling recommendations is one of the more disturbing aspects of sub-cultures. Senior executives are probably not aware of the number of recommendations that are set aside, but if they can remember their own journey through the ranks it would probably not surprise them that this issue does exist. The sub-culture where ideas get lost is the domain of the But-Heads. A But-Head is someone who listens to a recommendation and dismisses it almost immediately. But-Heads are idea blockers. You have probably heard any number of the following in your own career:

- Great idea, **BUT**, the boss would not let that happen.

- Great idea, **BUT**, we could not get the money to do that.

- Great idea, **BUT**, now is not the time to approach anyone on this.

- Great idea, **BUT**, I think we should try my idea first.

- Great idea, **BUT**, it would not go well with your peers.

- Great idea, **BUT**, we have other more important issues to worry about.

- Great idea, **BUT**, we could not get (Department) to participate.

- Great idea, **BUT**, it just wouldn't work around here.

It can really be discouraging working for, or with, a But-Head. Some of the more talented people in your organization can become very discouraged if what they think is a good idea gets tossed aside by a But-Head. Lean can get at the recommendations that do not see the light of day because of But-Heads. Employees, working on self-directed teams (Kaizen) will at least have their ideas heard by someone outside the influence of their most immediate superior. Lean facilitators who are also Lean thinkers would never dismiss a recommendation with a BUT.

If a recommendation has merit it will be pursued. If a recommendation is not appropriate for the problem at hand, a discussion, perhaps using the 5-Why theory, could help the person with the recommendation understand why it will not work. Discussing alternative ideas and keeping that person involved in an alternative solution will keep that individual onboard.

We have facilitated many Kaizen events where someone receiving the Lean training stated that Lean sounded great but they will never get their boss to do what needs to get done. Further investigation frequently reveals a But-Head. In these situations we hold fast in our resolve to challenge those who resist change. Whether it's a Concrete Head or a But-Head we are there to send the message that change is inevitable.

Lean establishes a great environment for workers who are talented and want to participate in change. Lean, as it should be, is a nightmare for those who do not want to change.

An aggressive plan with exhaustive participation by senior executives is an effective method to get at the subcultures and informal processes. The education and involvement of every employee in your organization will also work to reduce the negative impact on your Lean implementation program. Those who really want change will get onboard, and the apathy, or destructive behavior, should be reduced significantly. Avoid planning paralysis. We come in contact with numerous companies who are planning a Lean transformation. Many of these companies are so caught up in the planning that they can not get the program started. In some cases, we are still communicating with companies that contacted us over a year ago. This is very frustrating because it is an indication that management is not committed to the Lean transformation and has delegated the responsibility for Lean so deep in their organizations that the glacial-paced cross-functional aspects of change are controlling the transformation.

If you are a CEO who has decided to transform your business to Lean, a good rule to follow is that your organization should be active in Kaizen activity within three months from the date that you committed to become Lean. This should allow plenty time for the initial training and planning activity. If your organization is not performing Kaizen activity at the end of three months, you need to get involved and determine why. Stalling out the implementation of Lean is a common strategy of those in the organization who do not want change. This could be the first test of your resolve.

Planning is a critical factor in preparing for a transformation. True Lean success will remain elusive unless there is a clear roadmap and everyone is traveling on the same path.

13

Executive Commit-ment

It is a terrible thing to look over your shoulder when you are trying to lead-and find no one there.
- Franklin D. Roosevelt.

Lean is the only option! This is the commitment and pronouncement that management must make to the entire company. A totally new culture must be created. Announcing change and maintaining your old methods, will send a negative message to the workforce. Lean has to be handled like an addiction; you have to admit that your current business processes are broken before you can expect a sincere effort to change. Anything short of this commitment will extend the timeline for implementation, or derail the program entirely.

It is critical that management discontinue operating policies that are counter to Lean concepts. As an example; metrics placing the priority on productivity should be replaced with metrics relating to inventory reduction and on-time delivery.

In our prior roles as internal Lean facilitators, we were constantly confronted with operating practices that were opposite to good Lean strategy. Productivity was the order of the day as was the monthly revenue target. Note that on-time delivery was not the top priority. The plants met the productivity and revenue requirements any way they could. Every plant was loaded with inventory that nobody wanted. Late orders with corresponding negative customer satisfaction issues were abundant. Creative accounting was employed to limit the abuse a plant manager would take if he missed the monthly revenue goal. On-time delivery percentage was the final hammer-blow that a plant manager could receive. However, this was an absurd measure from operations where plant managers were often times directed by Division executives to ship large orders ahead of the smaller older orders in an attempt to make the revenue targets.

When transitioning from traditional operating philosophies to Lean, one of the more difficult issues, that will truly test your commitment, is the change in focus from revenue and profits to quality and delivery.

We are aware that revenue and profits are critical. However, revenue and profit should be the result of processes that are based on delivering value to the end customer. If you are successful in this change of focus you should surpass historical revenue and profit performance levels. Here are just a few "never do" items that you should keep in mind if you are the CEO and want a speedy and successful Lean implementation.

- If your Lean plan calls for a certain activity, you should never be the reason why that activity did not take place.

- Do not allow, or give anyone in your company, a reason to delay a Lean activity.

- If you have a negative thought about a specific Lean activity or result, never express your displeasure in front of those individuals who participated in the Kaizen event. This does not mean that you should not urge them to do better.

- Never fail to acknowledge even the smallest success.

- Never fail to do as you say.

Managers need to become Lean thinkers. Discuss proposed activity, or spending, in terms of value, and avoid any activity, or spending, that is not substantiated by a valid Lean principle. We are aware of one plant where a proposal to renew a three-year lease for a fleet of forklift trucks was nearly approved, until a Lean thinker asked why the proposal should be approved when every effort would be made in the future to eliminate the need for most of those vehicles.

As the CEO, the likely test of your commitment to Lean will come from those who hold the highest positions in your company. Some key players will likely think that the program is for others, and that they, and their respective organizations, are certainly not the problem. The object of Lean is to create and promote change; as our chapter on the process of change suggests, those in your company who embrace change from the outset will be in the minority.

In our prior roles as internal Lean facilitators, we were constantly confronted with operating practices that were opposite to good Lean strategy. Productivity was the order of the day as was the monthly revenue target. Note that on-time delivery was not the top priority. The plants met the productivity and revenue requirements any way they could. Every plant was loaded with inventory that nobody wanted. Late orders with corresponding negative customer satisfaction issues were abundant. Creative accounting was employed to limit the abuse a plant manager would take if he missed the monthly revenue goal. On-time delivery percentage was the final hammer-blow that a plant manager could receive. However, this was an absurd measure from operations where plant managers were often times directed by Division executives to ship large orders ahead of the smaller older orders in an attempt to make the revenue targets.

When transitioning from traditional operating philosophies to Lean, one of the more difficult issues, that will truly test your commitment, is the change in focus from revenue and profits to quality and delivery.

We are aware that revenue and profits are critical. However, revenue and profit should be the result of processes that are based on delivering value to the end customer. If you are successful in this change of focus you should surpass historical revenue and profit performance levels. Here are just a few "never do" items that you should keep in mind if you are the CEO and want a speedy and successful Lean implementation.

- If your Lean plan calls for a certain activity, you should never be the reason why that activity did not take place.

- Do not allow, or give anyone in your company, a reason to delay a Lean activity.

- If you have a negative thought about a specific Lean activity or result, never express your displeasure in front of those individuals who participated in the Kaizen event. This does not mean that you should not urge them to do better.

- Never fail to acknowledge even the smallest success.

- Never fail to do as you say.

Managers need to become Lean thinkers. Discuss proposed activity, or spending, in terms of value, and avoid any activity, or spending, that is not substantiated by a valid Lean principle. We are aware of one plant where a proposal to renew a three-year lease for a fleet of forklift trucks was nearly approved, until a Lean thinker asked why the proposal should be approved when every effort would be made in the future to eliminate the need for most of those vehicles.

As the CEO, the likely test of your commitment to Lean will come from those who hold the highest positions in your company. Some key players will likely think that the program is for others, and that they, and their respective organizations, are certainly not the problem. The object of Lean is to create and promote change; as our chapter on the process of change suggests, those in your company who embrace change from the outset will be in the minority.

14

Executive Participation

Leadership is action, not position.
- Donald H. McGannon

Management must commit to active and frequent participation in the transformation process. Issuing memos and one-time speeches will not provide adequate evidence that management desires change. You have to get out onto the production floor, and into the administrative offices, and participate in the change process. You must make the Lean transition the number one priority.

A good way to jumpstart your Lean program is to establish minimums relative to the time each executive must spend involved in the Lean transition. Each executive in your company should participate in at least one Kaizen event within three months from the start of implementation.

A CEO of one company, that has been very successful in implementing Lean, required evidence from each direct report that he or she had at least twelve hours of direct participation in the Lean transformation each month. There were no exceptions to this rule, and each executive had to provide details of their participation in the Lean implementation for the following month. We subscribe wholeheartedly to this approach.

If you think this approach is overkill, consider the implications of lesser efforts. Lean will become the program of the month very quickly if executives are not visible during the transition. Kaizen events will lack the energy, and urgency, required to provide Lean solutions. Employees at all levels will fabricate reasons why they can not afford to take the time to participate in Kaizen events.

In the three plus years that Keith facilitated Kaizen events at his prior company, there was only one Kaizen team that had a senior executive present. As a result, he was constantly quizzed by participants as to the commitment of senior management. There was a real "we/they" issue in that company.

Planning Kaizen events at this company was a real nightmare. There was no single instance where Keith did not have to beg, borrow, or steal employees to participate in events. The only issue that caused local plant management any concern was that there was a corporate mandate for Lean and that a total refusal to participate might cause them problems. This did not mean that they would not do everything in their power to limit their exposure to the program.

The real issue at this company was that the CEO chose to discriminate with regard to the aspects of Lean that he wanted to focus on. He wanted the low hanging fruit that was available from certain types of Kaizen events. However, the Lean implementation effort could never be an excuse for missing productivity, or revenue, targets. The CEO failed to trust in the very program that he claimed to want implemented. He did not want to risk a few months focusing entirely on Lean. He somehow expected that the Lean facilitators would be able to create a Lean operation amongst the chaos. Plant managers understood this low hanging fruit strategy, and would support Kaizen events planned in the production area. However, any attempt to get at the non-production processes was met with a high level of resistance.

As a final note we offer this. A lack of executive commitment and participation acts like a virus on the Lean body that you are attempting to create, yet it provides the lifeblood for the "Concrete Heads". Concrete heads are out there waiting for you to waiver, just a tiny bit, in your resolve. They are in your organization acting as the advance guard for your doomed program. The reason these concrete heads can be so effective is that they are more visible, and communicate more frequently with the workforce, than the average executive.

Preventing the influence of concrete heads, along with executive involvement will help to prevent Lean from becoming elusive.

15

Lean Accounting

You can circle your wagons around any accountant who understands and aspires to Lean concepts.
- Keith Gilpatrick

In this chapter we will review the two aspects of accounting that will change as you get further into a Lean transforma tion. First is the role that accountants play in everyday operations, and second, the accounting and reporting for manufacturing operations.

Accountants

Accountants, who understand Lean, can contribute greatly to your Lean transformation program. Accountants are involved directly or indirectly with everything that is done to transact business. They oversee the budget process and are the custodians of enterprise funds. Mostly everything done to transform your operation to Lean will have an accounting element.

The need for accounting personnel to be totally familiar with Lean theory may appear obvious to the reader. However, it is our experience, that in practice, accounting and accountants have received very little attention.

In our prior company, the accountants were so busy participating in non-value-added activity that it was rare to see one on a Kaizen team. In many instances we held formal meetings with accounting department personnel to educate them on Lean and solicit their participation in the Lean transformation program. While the individuals we met with were enthused about Lean theory, they would give us a puppy look followed by comments suggesting that we could not possibly be working for the same company. The genesis for this response was corporate mandates that were counter to good Lean practice. As stated earlier, the company's approach to Lean was very selective. The company wanted to get at the low-hanging fruit that was available from balancing production and eliminating people, but did very little to promote eliminating waste from other business processes, change policies and procedures, or change performance metrics to conform to Lean theory.

In a properly executed Lean transformation the accounting department plays a major role. The chief accountant would be among the first to receive Lean training and should be a key participant in the development of the Lean plan. The aspects of Lean that should get the chief accountants attention immediately are the elimination of waste from all processes and the Flow and Pull elements. Once the theory is explained, no one person in the company would be more aware of the waste in processes, and the positive implications of implementing Flow and Pull in the manufacturing operations.

Accounting and Reporting for Non-Manufacturing Operations

Our focus for now will be on the elimination of waste from non-manufacturing processes. We will discuss Flow and Pull for manufacturing later in this chapter.

As mentioned earlier, the typical authorization matrix and supporting policies and procedures represent the control aspects of the business and are responsible for a big part of the waste that exists in administrative processes. Tasked with the fiscal responsibility for the company, the chief accountant is conscious of the need for control. As a key player in the implementation of Lean, he or she would see the need to eliminate the non-value-added effort that is generated as a result of those control requirements.

In the typical business, the authorization matrix is a component of the overall financial operating policies and procedures. The accounting department should be tasked with the responsibility of reviewing and maintaining the integrity of those policies and procedures as the company moves through the Lean transformation. In many cases there can be a financial component to an operations policy and procedure. In these cases, cross-functional cooperation will be critical to maintaining the integrity of those operating procedures.

In addition to the authorization matrix issues, the chief accountant is primarily responsible for most of the reporting performed in the enterprise. After receiving Lean training, the chief accountant's perspective on reporting should change. The chief accountant should address the pertinence and frequency of reports from a value-added perspective and be vigilant in his or her attempts to accomplish reporting in a timely manner. The pertinence of reporting relates primarily to the reporting of manufacturing operations and will be discussed in that section. One of the primary goals of the accounting function must be to review every report currently being prepared and determine if the subject matter covered is consistent with Lean theory. For example; the company would not want to continue reporting results based on performance metrics that are not Lean based.

We have said that cross-functional cooperation will become a necessity in a successful Lean transformation. This was pointed out specifically in the brief summary of the DFMA concept. Accounting should play a major role in the program to broaden cross-functional cooperation. The chief accountant's broad knowledge of company operations will be useful in the planning stage of the Lean transformation. Once Kaizen activity begins, participation by accounting personnel can provide the team with a broad knowledge of business operations in the preparation and presentation of the current process flow.

Planning

Planning the Lean transition is a difficult task. Once the senior executives have received Lean training, they must apply the concepts to prepare for future operations. Almost every aspect of operations, as they existed prior to the Lean transformation, will change. At the core of these old operations are the operating/capital budgets and the financial/operating policies and procedures. These represent the methods that will be employed to accomplish the overall strategic plan. It is the strategic plan that is being changed, and, because of this, the budgets and operating policies and procedures will need to change. Here again, the sequence of events will vary based on the priorities that are established by senior management. With this, we will focus on key elements of the transition that will impact the core components and not worry about when they might occur. In each case there will be a direct link to the domain of the chief accountant that supports our contention that he or she should be a key player in the transformation.

- **Machinery and Equipment** – It is likely that the nature of spending relative to machinery and equipment will change. You would be wise to review the capital budget and defer machinery and equipment purchases that support old process theory. Buying another large metal stamping machine for example would not be recommended if your new process demands smaller and slower machinery. A good TPM program will also have a positive impact on planned spending for machinery and equipment. The useful life of equipment is likely to be extended.

- **Plant or Plant Expansion** – Plans to expend funds on new plants or plant expansions should be deferred. It is likely that employing Lean theory to the current plant layout, and existing production processes, will recapture plant space and planned additions or expansions may not be necessary. If you take a very aggressive approach to inventory reduction, the elimination of your current warehouse facility can save a tremendous amount of space that could be used to accommodate future plant expansion. The plans for expansion may change once the full benefits from a Lean transition are understood. If your business currently operates from multiple plant locations there is a possibility that you may be able to consolidate operations and vacate certain facilities.

- **Research and Development/Design Engineering** – A candid appraisal of Value and the Value Stream is likely to change the R&D/Design Engineering components of operations. Changes to the strategic plan that arise from a Lean vision will likely change the focus of these operations. The chief accountant would be the likely third party, at the executive level, to coordinate the cross-functional aspects of these changes.

- **Training** – The focus of training is likely to change. Take this opportunity to redirect your program for continuing education and support an aggressive plan for culture change. Replace plans to send employees to seminars, which satisfy individual education goals, with a Lean education. Combine that with a project completion requirement so that you receive a direct and timely benefit from your education spending.

- **Organization** – The strategic plan should consider what the organization will look like in yearly increments out to five years. If value is engineered into the product and assembly techniques it is likely that the size of your current quality department will change. Also, if quality is engineered into the product and production processes, there could be a substantial impact on the production engineering department. The strategic plan should ultimately aim at flattening the organization by reducing the layers of management between the CEO and the plant workers. The value stream mapping that occurs early in the transformation process should provide the data necessary for future organizational changes. Executives with vision and a determination to eliminate all non-value-added effort will create strategic and tactical plans that will significantly reduce the costs associated with administering the business process.

- **Labor Relations** – In some business enterprises, the chief accountant will oversee the legal and human resource departments. In this capacity he or she will need to be very visible during the planning phase. If there are labor unions, the company will have to take particular care not to alienate them and jeopardize the current contract or the prospects for continued cooperation.

- **Treasury Function** – In his or her capacity as the custodian of corporate funds the chief accountant and his or her accounting personnel have been dealing directly with the quality aspects of the products and services offered by the company. Putting aside the trend in most industries for customers to stretch out payments to suppliers, quality issues are more than likely the reason why cash is not collected in a timely manner. Most cash collection functions act as the intermediaries between the customer and the production or service departments that produced the products or provided the service. If there is anything wrong with the product or service provided, cash collection personnel find themselves in the middle of dispute with no real mandate to settle the issue in a timely fashion. In this respect, the chief accountant has a horse in the race and will want to insure that the plan for future operations will create processes that reduce the quality issues and provide seamless solutions so that customers are not given reasons to delay cash payments.

- **Metrics** – Metrics will play a major role in measuring and reporting the progress that you are making with your Lean transformation. The first step in providing a feedback process is the establishment of Lean goals. Once you have determined these goals, you will be able to create a series of metrics that will establish your starting point and then report performance once the implementation program has begun. On occasion, the first thing that you need to do to in order to improve is take a step back. Metrics are an example of this. Historically, most senior executives have not wanted to get caught-up in the minutia of the business processes. Senior executives have relied on metrics that report the status of major segments of operations such as inventory turns, days sales outstanding, return of investment, etc. The planning phase of the Lean implementation requires that these major segments be broken down into metrics that tell the complete story. Taking the days sales outstanding metric as an example; the planning metrics would likely include the following:

Number of late invoices and their total value by reason code;

a) Short shipment

b) Wrong product shipped

c) Damaged shipment

d) Late shipment

e) Shipped to incorrect location

f) Incorrect invoice

g) Product did not pass incoming inspection

h) Service as performed did not solve problem

i) Service was not satisfactory

j) Wrong product ordered

Once you have detailed all of the reasons why cash is not collected on a timely basis, you can plan improvement activities to determine the root cause of each, and report the status of that activity until the problem is no longer an issue. As a senior executive, your commitment to the Lean transformation will be tested in the early phases of the transition. You need to start at this level in order to plan an effective transformation. Identifying and permanently fixing the problems is your goal.

As we stated earlier, accounting deals with every aspect of your business. Accounting should play a major role in developing metrics that will establish your starting point and report the status of your improvement program.

By now, we hope you see that accounting involvement is vital to the Lean transformation planning process. Without the direct participation by accounting, Lean is not just elusive, it is probably not attainable.

Kaizen

It is our experience that almost every Kaizen event will have one or more accounting issues that will arise. Without someone from that organization on the team you will create lists of issues that will have to be addressed by accounting in order to validate your understanding of accounting issues associated with the process that you are reviewing. This is particularly true in the non-manufacturing Kaizen events. Non-manufacturing Kaizen events will generally fall within two categories; events covering financial administration; and events covering the administration of direct manufacturing support operations such as, design engineering, production engineering, purchasing, quality, etc. Financial administration Kaizen events should be planned and administered by the accounting department. Direct manufacturing support Kaizen events should have at least one accounting department representative on the team.

Earlier, we cautioned you regarding the accuracy of the process maps depicting the current process. Process mapping is a critical phase of the Kaizen event and it is in your best interest to complete that step quickly and accurately so that the majority of the time spent during the event can be used creating the new process. Keep in mind also, that no Kaizen team should be made up entirely of workers from the process that is being reviewed. The Kaizen process provides a system of checks and balances that should eliminate suggestions that one organization in the company has more influence than others. While accountants have gotten the reputation associated with the term "Bean Counters," it is interesting to see the results you will get when those accountants are members of teams reviewing manufacturing operations. Likewise, it is interesting to see how well those accountants react to having non-financial people in the majority on a team reviewing financial administration processes.

Accounting and Reporting for Manufacturing Operations

The Standard Cost System, which was created to provide a method of allocating overhead costs to inventory, measures the efficiency of production operations, and provides a base from which products are priced, is rendered useless in a Lean environment. While standard cost is necessary for tax and financial reporting purposes, it should not be the accounting system used to report the effectiveness of a Lean operation. Lean manufacturing requires Lean management accounting. If you accept the premise that a substantial amount of the activity performed in a typical manufacturing operation is non-value added and should be discontinued, you will be looking for an alternative to your standard cost system for performance reporting purposes.

Perhaps the best approach to take in explaining the need for something other than standard costs is to imagine a Lean production cell that is perfectly balanced, using point-of-use inventory storage, producing and packing for shipment only on actual demand from the customer, ordering replenishment materials and assemblies using an electronic Kanban system. Unlike the traditional production line, the Lean cell uses customer orders only to commence and control production and is otherwise paperless, eliminating most of the transaction waste that is prevalent in the traditional system. In addition, the quality delivered from the Lean cell will be much higher than the traditional production line once the company has adopted DFMA and builds quality into the process and the product. Using the traditional standard cost system, this Lean cell would be subject to overhead allocations that are not totally applicable to that operation. Variances reported as part of the standard cost system would more than likely be negative because the cell will produce products based on actual demand rather than produce products based on an MRP system that is designed to maximize production using actual orders and forecasted demand.

Allocating Overhead Costs to Inventory

Aside from the fact that the overhead allocations would probably not be fair with regard to the support costs associated with the Lean cell, traditional manufacturing companies with very low inventory turns will go to great lengths to maximize the costs that can be allocated to on hand inventory and are thus deferred and kept off the profit and loss statement. When your transformation is complete, using a paperless Kanban system, you could have multiple turns each month with hardly any inventory on hand to value, and you will have no need for the people who are needed to process and control a large inventory. The space needed to produce in a Lean production cell will be much less than a traditional production process. Once the entire plant is Lean a lot of space should be vacant which would distort traditional overhead allocations that are based on occupancy costs.

Measuring Production Efficiency

All measurements associated with the efficiency of the Lean production cell will be visual, real time, measurements. On the hour, the cell will visually report how it is doing in relation to Takt Time and product quality. Any variance from Takt Time production will be posted in the cell with root cause analysis to explain any variation and indicate what the cell workers have done to prevent a reoccurrence. Because Lean cell workers are tasked with traditional indirect labor activities (Material replenishment, packing and shipping transactions, material handling, cleaning, preventive maintenance, machine change-over, etc.), the old standards based on having a worker busy producing product would not be appropriate.

Pricing Products

Using standard cost to price products and report margins in traditional manufacturing operations is at best a crapshoot. Unless you have the best standard cost system that is maintained and adjusted on a real time basis, which would defeat the purpose of the standard cost system, the accuracy of the information attained would be questionable. Using Lean production cells throughout your manufacturing operation should generate cost data that is more reliable. It makes no sense to have products absorb costs that are not applicable to the process that was used to create them.

Activity Based Costing (ABC) is probably a better method of accounting for Lean production activity. In our past experience, variations of ABC costing have been attempted with varying results. ABC costing can require more hands-on activity to develop and maintain but will provide more accurate data. The one thing that we would caution against is creating separate systems for fiscal and operational reporting. These combination systems are typically loaded with wasteful, non- value added activities. A book could be written to cover this single aspect of the Lean transformation. For the purposes of this book we feel that accounting issues can be a contributor to the elusiveness of Lean and have pointed out our major concerns. Selecting the accounting process that you will use to report operations should be a planning consideration, and little should be done with regard to the implementation of Lean until this issue is resolved.

Having reviewed what we feel are the important Lean considerations relative to accounting and accounting department personnel, we would have to add that the success of your Lean implementation relative to these issues is based solely on the ability of the accountants to accept the propositions supporting Lean theory. The task ahead for the accountants is to stand firm on their fiscal responsibility, and, at the same time, accept that the methods currently in place to provide fiscal control are as outdated as the traditional mass-manufacturing processes.

The target is, and always will be, waste. The accounting organization should not be excluded from participation in the process, nor should the accounting organization feel than their fiscal control processes should be excluded from the scrutiny of good Lean thinking.

Lean is truly elusive if accounting personnel do not participate.

16

Final Thoughts

There isn't a plant or business on earth that couldn't
stand a few improvements-and be better for them.
Someone is going to think of them. Why not beat
the other fellow to it.

- Roger W. Babson

What we hoped to accomplish with this book was to
provide a quick and basic study of Lean; provide
compelling reasons for change; discuss the change
process; alert the reader to the Lean Math and Cost of Quality
issues; offer a comparison of Lean and Six-Sigma; and provide
insight to the importance of education, planning, management
commitment, and management participation. Finally, we
wanted to show the cultures and formal/informal systems that
can exist in companies that have not taken a critical look at
themselves for an extended period of time.

The spirit and tone of this book was created from our combined 70+years of experience in global business operations. This book was intended to be a candid look at business as we have experienced it, and, in certain cases, we have drawn broad conclusions regarding the typical batch and queue manufacturing operations based on our experience, as well conversations with friends, colleagues and associates who have worked in other companies in the United States and around the world. Again, we are not human behavior scientists but we are humans who have been subjected to the behavior of numerous types of executives that, for good or bad, are responsible for thoughts presented in this book regarding management. We believe most companies that have not taken a critical look at their operating and management philosophies need to do so. Waste is prevalent in most business operations, and Lean is the best solution we have found to attack waste and provide value to the customers who purchase products and services.

We hope this book will inspire those who read it to think about change and look to Lean as the vehicle that will drive the change process. We view Lean as a possible alternative program to outsourcing, or to seeking suppliers who are located in perceived low cost countries. We are confident that those who successfully implement Lean will be effective competitors in the global marketplace with products that are the best in quality, offer the best total cost, and can be delivered at the time they are needed.

Operating in the country where you hope to attain a substantial market share is a wise decision. Doing so while applying Lean concepts and being properly prepared, is even wiser. Try to temper the internal, and external, pressure to relocate, or source offshore, with a need to do it correctly, and with accurate financial and risk data.

The issues we have addressed in this book are those which are the major contributors to "The Elusive Lean Enterprise". By focusing on those issues you will greatly enhance your chances of success. The reward is worth the effort and the results will surprise you, if you implement Lean correctly. There are many instances where companies have faltered, where Lean remains elusive. Those who have had great success will tell you that there is never-ending opportunity with Lean.

Glossary of Commonly-Used Lean Terminology

5 Why's

A method of getting to the root-cause of problems. The theory is that the first reason given for why something didn't work is rarely the real root cause reason for failure. This tool is particularly useful during Kaizen events where the majority of the team is not familiar with the process. Every step is the process should be challenged and the 5-why method is a great way to get the job done.

5S The basic principles of a 5S program are to create an organized and clean work area. Taken to the plant level, 5S creates a spotless plant that has excellent lighting, reduces wasted people movement, is safe, and allows nothing in the plant that isn't needed. 5S = Separate, Sort, Sweep, Standardize, and Sustain

Activity Based Costing A management accounting system that assigns costs based on the resources used to manufacture an item. Contrast this with the Standard Cost System.

Andon A visual control device, usually a light panel or light post, to signal the status of a machine or inventory. If the light is green, everything is OK. If the light is yellow, there is a material issue (the machine is empty). If the light is red, something is wrong with the machine (a machine malfunction or a material feed issue).

Autonomation Using people in concert with machines to error-proof a process. One application of this tool is a light post (Andon) that will show green if everything is OK, yellow if the machine needs material or red to indicate that the machine has stopped because it has detected something wrong with itself or the material being processed.

Batch-and-Queue Mass production philosophy of processing in large batches and sending those batches on to the next downstream process.

Best Practice To determine the most efficient method of performing an operation or process and passing that method on the others, thus avoiding a repetition of the learning experience at other locations.

Chaku-chaku The Japanese words for a Rabbit Chase process

Changeover To change a Tool, Die, Paint, or Mold/Casting. The changeover must be made so that a new part can be produced. The Lean objective is to change the tool in ten minutes or less.

Concrete Head An individual, who for whatever reason, does not want to embrace the Lean Enterprise concepts.

DFMA Design for Manufacturing and Assembly. Design engineering theory and techniques which are used to ensure that the final design will assemble easily, and will be made using fewer parts that are readily available at the best price. A good DFMA program can produce significant reductions in production time, material costs, and production engineering support.

Flow To have product flow through all processes one piece at a time, and at the rate (Takt-Time) demanded by the downstream customer. This requires the balancing of work for each person or machine in the production process and requires that the distance that material and people travel be dramatically reduced. Standard Work must be implemented as part of the Flow system.

Focused Factory   A plant layout that has production cells that include all of the equipment and personnel needed to make a particular product or series of products. A modified version of the Focused Factory can be established in cases where one or more machines are used to satisfy parts or assemblies for multiple products. Metal stamping and painting are good examples of machines or processes that may be used on each product regardless of its product family.

Heijunka   Heijunka is a Japanese term that means leveled production.

Institutionalizing Lean - 14 steps:

1. Management education and commitment followed by engagement.

2. Management must clearly communicate the plan, the reason for it and, to the extent possible, outline the future following implementation.

3. Policy Deployment must support Lean goals.

4. Educate everyone in the organization.

5. Lean must be the only system allowed. A real culture change must take place.

6. People must be given authority to make changes.

7. Concrete heads must be removed.

8. Management must stay focused and understand the transition phases.

9. Avoid Hysteresis.

10. Tools applied to the whole organization.

11. All improvements must be recognized.

12. No embarrassment or retribution for admitting problems.

13. Be innovative and creative.

14. Make it fun!

Jidoka The Japanese word for improving quality by fool-proofing a process.

Just-in-time (JIT) A system where materials are delivered to a production plant or production cell in time for use. The objective is to reduce inventory throughout the process and not pay carrying costs for inventory that is not needed.

KAIZEN A three to five day project to review and make changes to a process. The project is performed by a self-directed team of 6 to 8 employees from different functional departments, with specific Lean goals to guide their work. The cycle followed in performing Kaizen is sometimes referred to as, Plan-Do-Check-Act. Additionally, identifying and eliminating Waste in a process is a constant goal of Kaizen. Kaizen is a dramatic process. In a normal Kaizen event a team designs and creates a production cell that will produce on-piece-at-a-time. They will actually change the location of manufacturing equipment, tools, people, and inventory to accommodate one-piece-flow. The administrative Kaizen event is just as dramatic. Again a team of employees will design and create a process that is void of waste and includes only process steps and people who add value to the downstream customer.

Kanban

Kanban is a signal for demand of specific product, in specific quantities, to be delivered to a specific process. Kanban is a critical element of the Pull system. Each Kanban is sized differently to meet the replenishment requirements and capabilities of the upstream suppliers so that the downstream customer will always have adequate supply and can meet fluctuating customer demand.

Lead Time

The time from the point when an order for material is sent to a supplier until the materials are received and available for use.

Line Balancing

A program where each process step is timed, recorded and presented on a frequency chart with the intent to balance the work so that each process step takes about the same amount of time to complete. The purpose of Line balancing is to determine the time it takes for a single completed piece of product to be manufactured so that the rate can be compared to the actual customer demand.

Line Balance Chart   A Pareto chart that depicts each process in a production line and the amount of time, expressed in seconds that each process takes. Using the Line Balance Chart you compare the longest production process time with the Takt Time to see if the line can meet the current demand of customers. The chart will also indicate where processes can be combined and still be performed as fast as the slowest process. This allows you to take people out of the process and still meet demand. Combining this tool with the U-Shaped Production Cell will enable you to better balance the work and create new assembly processes.

Material Travel Must Be Limited   The distance that material travels through the process must be limited. Each production process should be located as close to the next downstream process as is practical. Point of use inventory storage should be a goal to eliminate the costs involved in managing and controlling inventory. If you bought material it should be delivered immediately to the machine or person who will use it to manufacture the product. Single-piece-flow requires that the downstream process be within easy reach. If the material has to travel large distances it should be triggered by a Kanban signal so that the amount of WIP inventory can be limited.

Monument

A machine or processes that are designed to produce large batches. Lean attempts to improve the capabilities of the machines or processes so that one-piece-flow can be established.

MRP

Material Requirements Planning is a program used to create requisitions for production materials. The program is based on current customer order backlog plus forecasted sales of finished products. The program calculates the material requirements to build the finished goods and compares that data with on hand inventory and creates requisitions to order needed materials. The quantities ordered are based on the future need plus safety stock and considers lead-time from suppliers.

One-Piece-Flow

A proven theory that assembling one piece at a time is faster than producing in batches. Additionally, using this method can detect quality problems early in the process and prevent costly rework. The one-piece method is instrumental in the line balancing process and will enable you to pace production to meet customer demand.

People Travel Must Be Limited   People movement, both hands and feet, should be limited to the extent practical. Material from the upstream process should be within easy reach and the components needed for the current production step should be within easy reach and organized in the sequence in which they are to be used. Tools needed in the production process should be within easy reach and should always be returned to their designated storage areas.

Perfection
To strive to be the best at everything you do. To use Kaizen and provide continuous incremental improvement. To constantly challenge how things are done and improve the quality of all products.

Place the Responsibility for Education low in the organization
Everyone in the organization must have a Lean education. When you have successfully completed the Lean transformation, supervisors and self-directed teams of employees will be responsible for ongoing Lean training.

Poka-Yoke
A part of a broader system of error proofing processes called Jidoka. Lean thinkers are constantly seeking ways to error proof processes. Techniques like the use of limit switches prevent items from being manufactured out of specification. Machines with built in stop mechanisms that prevent waste/scrap because of the misplacement of materials or components into machines. The primary purpose of Poka-yoke is to prevent costly inspection and rework, and to make the end product friendly to the user.

Policy Deployment   To create and implement operating policies that meets the goals of the Lean Enterprise transformation. Inventory turns of 24, a 30 % reduction in direct labor, eliminate the current warehouse, or a 15 % improvement in profit after tax, are examples of goals that one might set. The policies would be to establish Flow and Pull systems in manufacturing using point-of-use inventory storage.

Process   A collection of individual operations necessary to produce something. Includes both people and machine operations.

Process Mapping   Process flow diagrams or charts that depict each step in a process as well as the number of people in that process and the numbers and types of documents currently used to control the process. The process map is used to help the Kaizen team identify value added, non-value added and non-value added but required processes, and establishes a time estimate for the current process.

Pull   To pull product through the entire production process in quantities, and at a rate, demanded by the downstream customer. Basically, if there is no demand for the product or if the demand slows then the production line stops or slows down to meet the situation. Pull starts at final assembly when a customer order is received and ends at your supplier location.

Rabbit Chase A production technique that has individual production workers performing each process in the production line to completely assemble a finished product. Using this technique a plant can vary the rate of production to meet non-linear customer demand.

Right-sized-tooling/machine To use a tool or machine that is sized to meet the production needs. Having a machine that can produce much faster that the process needs to work at is wasteful. Having a machine that cannot produce at the speed necessary is also wasteful.

Six-Sigma A scientific method for identifying the root-cause of problems in both manufacturing and administrative processes. While not a specific element or tool emerging from the Toyota Production System, Six-Sigma compliments Lean Enterprise. Implemented and run properly the Flow system will find and eliminate process variations that may cause quality problems. Six-Sigma would be used when quality issues remain after Flow and other Lean techniques have been implemented.

SMED Single Minute Exchange of Dies, or quick changeover techniques, that will reduce the size of batches processed by large machines that currently have complicated tool and die changeover requirements. A successful SMED project will ultimately reduce inventory and speed-up or perhaps eliminate traditional batch-and-queue processes.

Spaghetti Charts A chart that depicts material and people movement in a production process. The chart also depicts the actual distance that material and people move to make a product. It is a valuable tool for Kaizen team members so that they can adequately represent the waste in the old process and reflect the efficiency created by the Kaizen event.

Spider Chart Also referred to as a Radar Chart in Excel. The chart is used to depict the current status of the Lean implementation or a specific aspect of the transformation, such as the 5S program.

Standard Costing The management accounting system that allocates operational costs based on machine hours or direct labor hours. This system rewards processes that work faster than the standard by reducing the per piece cost, but can cause the accumulation of large unwanted inventories.

Standard Work Each step in the process should be defined and must be performed repeatedly in the same manner. Variations in the process will create quality problems requiring costly rework or scrap. Standard Work will define the most efficient methods to produce product using available equipment, people, and material. The Standard Work depicts the key process points, operator procedures, production sequence, safety issues, and quality checks. Standard Work must identify the amount and location of WIP inventory in the cell. Developing Standard Work is one of the more difficult Lean disciplines. Once you start to implement Flow and Pull systems your workers can get caught-up in the dynamic changes and get behind in documenting those changes.

Takt-Time

The pace at which the production line needs to operate in order to meet the customer demand for product. Takt time is calculated by dividing the total time available for manufacturing for a period of time by the total customer demand for that same time period.

Throughput Time

The time it takes for a single item to travel through the complete process. In a single-piece-flow system, it is the total time for each process step and is much lower than the throughput time of a batch process system where a single part must wait for all other parts to be processed before it can move on to the next process.

TPM

A program for machine and tool maintenance that extends the useful life of equipment and ensures that equipment will be available when needed to produce product. A good TPM program will include maintenance procedures for all equipment operators as well as production cell workers **(Autonomous Maintenance)**. TPM should include scheduled preventive maintenance

U-Shaped Production Cells   A production line that has the form of a horseshoe. The Japanese have proven that a horseshoe shaped cell, moving product clockwise through the process is the most affective. People and machinery are placed close together allowing material to be handed to the next process, one piece at a time. In the typical straight-line production process there are large distances between machines and people which create piles of inventory and limit the ability of people in the line from helping others.

Value   Value, as expressed by the customer. The customer component has three dimensions; the external end customer; the downstream customer of any internal upstream process; and your company as the customer of external suppliers.

Value Selling   To have sales persons who are aware of the production capabilities of a company and be able to sell to customers in quantities that meet their short-term needs (JIT). To get customers to establish a Kanban system for products they order. This reduces the investment the customer has in their inventory and should be a major selling tool.

Value Stream   The entire series of processes that are used by a company to provide value to the customer. The Value Stream for each product or service offered by the company should be identified. The Value Stream is depicted through the use of detailed process flow diagrams/

charts that will ultimately be used to determine the Value Added components of the Value Stream as well as the Non-Value Added components. The process charts must depict the total number of steps taken to provide value as well as the number of people involved, the time taken to perform the process step, and all documents used.

Visual Workplace   Memos, charts, and graphs, available throughout the workplace, that present the current status of all operations compared with historical data and geared toward strategic and tactical Lean goals. Additionally, each production cell will have visual representations of its performance with regard to productivity, training, problem recognition and programs to solve those problems.

Cost of Quality Checklists

Prevention costs

O   Quality planning

O   Quality auditing

O   Vendor quality assurance

O   Design reviews

O   Process engineering (capability studies)

O   Development of test and measuring equipment

O   Quality training

- Certification of competence
- Analysis of quality data
- Quality improvement programs
- Preventive maintenance
- Maintenance of ISO 9000 Registration
- Calibration of measuring and test equipment
- Credit control
- Market research/customer surveys
- Process control
- Internal personal customer contact
- External personal customer contact
- Business planning
- Product qualification
- Value engineering
- Quality awareness materials
- Reliability/maintainability projections
- Contract reviews
- Failure mode and effect analysis
- Quality function development
- Early supplier involvement in design
- Total preventive maintenance
- Testing and field trials
- Project reviews
- Quality plans
- Clear work instructions

○ Visual work instructions

○ Effective meeting management

○ Kaizen events

○ Six Sigma project investigations

○ Design experiments

Appraisal costs

○ Goods receiving inspection

○ Inspection

○ Testing

○ Analysis of test and inspection results

○ Field testing

○ Laboratory testing

○ Materials consumed in inspection and test

○ Mandatory approvals and certification

○ Stock evaluation

○ Documentation checking and review

○ Set up inspection and test

○ Process surveillance / patrol inspection

○ Market surveys

○ Sample testing

○ Pre-delivery inspection

○ Pre-production verification

O   Record storage

O   Process audits

O   Design audits

O   Product audits

O   Literature audits

O   System audits

O   Proof reading

O   Prototyping

O   Bill of material audits

O   Inventory audits

O   Design cost estimating

O   Perpetual inventory verification

O   Credit checking

O   Data verification

Internal failure costs

○ Disruption costs

○ Rework / Repair

○ Recheck / Test

○ Scrap

○ Liability claims

○ Bad Debts/Loss of interest($) on delayed invoices

○ Employee time stealers

○ Loss of Process Capacity

○ Excess and Obsolete stockholding

○ Defect diagnosis

○ Machine downtime

○ Corrective maintenance

○ Concession reviews

○ Corrective design changes and modifications

○ Credit Note administration

○ Downgrading

○ Pre-Delivery retrofits

○ Redesign

○ Expediting

○ Excess employee turnover and absence

○ Failure mode and effect analysis

○ Failure analysis

○ Troubleshooting

- Unplanned Overtime
- Premium charge transportation costs
- Operator efficiency variance
- Premium charge for sub-contract parts
- Demurrage
- Waiting time
- Outdated computer systems
- Overtime worked due to rework
- Overtime worked due to process problems
- Specifications errors
- Field returns processing

External failure costs

- Complaint handling
- Warranty
- Product recall
- Product Liability Insurance
- Concessions
- Loss of sales
- Invoice error corrections
- Post-delivery or field retrofits
- Customer litigation
- Late delivery penalties

O Field service and repair

O Field returns

O Shipping/Delivery errors

O Premium freight costs

O Loss of Customer Goodwill

O Corrective action

O Disruption costs

O Free of Charge issues

O Compensation

O Lost interest

O Dispute negotiation

O Sales cancellations

O Cost of exceeding requirements

Cost of exceeding requirements

O Extra copies of documents

O Reports that are not needed

O Detail in written reports far in excess of recipients needs

O Detailed analytical effort and reporting when estimates would suffice

O Over engineered products

Cost of lost opportunity

- O Lost sales
- O Customers ordering competitors' products due to excessive Lead Time
- O Customers ordering competitors' products due to poor market reputation
- O Wrong products offered for a customer's specific application
- O Lack of product knowledge

Following are checklists by function that can also be used to help determine the true quality costs of any operation.

Sales and Marketing

- O Revisits to customers caused by bad original planning
- O Revising proposals and quotations due to errors or omissions
- O Correcting price lists, sales literature, software
- O Redefining order requirements after order has been entered
- O Clarifying or correcting errors in internal orders
- O Administration of product returns, warranty claims and complaints
- O Investigation of field problems
- O Answering customer problems and complaints
- O Resolving billing problems

○ Rescheduling jobs because of problems

○ Getting deviations approved by customers

○ Attending problem investigation meetings

○ Revising inaccurate market forecasts

○ Explaining schedule delays to customers

○ Recovering lost customer confidence

○ Product liability defense

○ Pro-forma invoice errors

○ Salesman not being trained

○ Lack of competitive knowledge

○ Poor pricing

○ Lack of timeliness in responding to customers

Engineering

○ Clarifying order or customer requirements

○ Correcting design errors

○ Correcting and revising design procedures

○ Preparing and processing change notices due to own problem

○ Changing drawings and specifications

○ Investigation and resolution of field/manufacturing problems

○ Rescheduling and revising project plans

- O Waiting time because of equipment downtime or late information

- O Investigating and resolving supplier problems

- O Processing concession requests

- O Product liability defense

- O Not meeting cost targets

- O Process capabilities studies

- O Tolerance studies

- O Interpreting field failure Data

- O Product spread/rationalization

- O Duplicated effort/design time

- O Material rationalization

- O Failure to apply lessons learned

- O Design for manufacture

Purchasing

O Clarifying and correcting inadequate drawing and specifications

O Correcting requisition errors

O Correcting purchase order errors

O Expediting and rescheduling

O Process deviation requests

O Liaison with suppliers on quality problems

O Correcting invoicing and payment errors

O Processing rejection paperwork

O Processing internally caused change notices

O Recovery costs associated with non-conforming material

O Waiting because of equipment downtime

O Dealing with claims for carrier or handling damage

O Travel to suppliers because of non-conformance issues

O Approving invoices due to incorrectly priced orders

O Processing concessions

O Helping suppliers reduce the cost of quality

O Reviewing slow moving / obsolete inventory

O Expediting deliveries due to non-payment or errors

O Purchasing obsolete parts

Manufacturing

- ○ Clarification of engineering requirements
- ○ Expediting and rescheduling
- ○ Correcting errors in manufacturing orders
- ○ Implementing changes not caused by customers
- ○ Dealing with missing or non-conforming material
- ○ Handling, documenting and reworking non-conforming material
- ○ Requesting deviations and concessions
- ○ Reworking/Retesting
- ○ Problem review meetings
- ○ Waiting due to equipment downtime
- ○ Rescheduling work due to poor forecasting
- ○ Rework and rescheduling due to design errors
- ○ Correcting poor workmanship
- ○ Investigating and correcting field problems
- ○ Processing rejected material paperwork
- ○ Rework and lost time due to inadequate machine capability
- ○ Correcting handling damage
- ○ Rework due to poor training or work instructions
- ○ Correcting incorrect reports
- ○ Processing extra work and reordering replacements for scrapped parts
- ○ Repairing equipment
- ○ Building and processing scrap material

- ○ Machine Maintenance
- ○ Building Repairs
- ○ Searching for correct issues of drawing and tapes
- ○ Clarifying inadequate work instructions

Quality Assurance

- ○ Evaluating suspect material
- ○ Firefighting problems
- ○ Issuing defect reports
- ○ Attending quality problem meetings
- ○ Investigating production and field failures
- ○ Problem solving with vendors
- ○ Monitoring and implementing corrective actions
- ○ Compiling and issuing analysis of defective material
- ○ Training and retraining of inspectors and operators
- ○ Unplanned overtime
- ○ Reissuing incorrect reports
- ○ Sorting Material
- ○ Correcting quality documents
- ○ Investigating test failures
- ○ Performing failure analysis
- ○ Tracing and purging discrepant material

Management Information Systems

○ Clarifying and correcting user requirements

○ Investigating and correcting inadequate service levels

○ Rescheduling and expediting work due to poor planning

○ Redefining projects due to poor project definition

○ Correcting problems caused by inadequately trained people

○ Correcting results of inadequate data backup and recovery procedures

○ Investigating and correcting operational problems

○ Waiting due to equipment downtime

○ Debugging operational programs and systems

○ Translating work due to lack of standard systems

○ Correcting database errors due to user mistakes

○ Inadequate long range system planning

○ Investigating and correcting supplier caused problems

○ Rerunning jobs because of problems

○ Issuing reports no-one needs or requires

○ Too much information

Human resources

O   Inability to flex workforce economically

O   Increasing or decreasing workforce due to poor forecasting

O   Correcting the results of poor, incomplete or inaccurate communications

O   Correcting the results of poor or inadequate training

O   Dealing with problems caused by poor supervision

O   Correcting errors in salary administration

O   Correcting errors in administration of benefits

O   Correcting errors in records and reports

O   Improving competence levels through training

O   Time lost through injury

Finance

○ Investigating and correcting billing problems

○ Investigating and correcting problems with supplier statements

○ Investigating problems and errors on expense reports

○ Revising forecasts because of delays, errors and failures

○ Investigating and correcting inventory errors

○ Processing engineering changes due to internal problems

○ Processing scrap, rework and excess labor costs

○ Waiting due to office equipment downtime or unavailability

○ Processing warranty claims and sales concessions

○ Correcting reports, forecasts and statements due to errors

○ Processing credit notes

○ Payroll analysis

○ Issuing reports no-one needs or requires

○ Dealing with unpaid suppliers

Field Service

○ False starts – lack of information or materials

○ Correction of manufacturing non-conformance

○ Waiting

○ Resolving billing problems

○ Obtaining complete information

○ Resolving questions of interpretation

○ Travel relating to non-conformance resolution

○ Attending meetings to discuss and resolve problems

Other quality costs

○ Interest on overdue receivables

About the Authors

Brian Furlong is the co-owner and Executive Vice President of Program Development of Lean Enterprise Inc.. He is co-author of the acclaimed Lean Mastery, Lean Office, Lean for Healthcare and Establishing Offshore Operations WBT courses. He is a seasoned, senior executive with 30 years experience in manufacturing and finance. Brian has worked for major multi-national companies such as Emerson, Westinghouse Invensys and National Westminster Bank. Throughout his career, he has developed in-depth knowledge of a wide variety of manufacturing and administrative processes.

As a former VP of Operations, he has managed multi-site domestic and international locations and has directed projects to start up plants in England, Ireland, Thailand and Mexico. Brian has also completed acquisitions in England, China and India.

Brian works with a number of Universities, corporations and organizations today to develop and delver cutting edge courses in both traditional and on-line formats. He is a frequent keynote speaker at conferences, association events and executive leadership seminars.

He is a passionate advocate of Lean Enterprise, having successfully completed transformations in numerous facilities in the United States, Mexico, Europe and Asia.

Keith Gilpatrick is President of Lean Enterprise Inc. Keith is co-author of the acclaimed Lean Mastery Suite of WBT courses, Lean Office, Lean for Healthcare and Establishing Offshore Operations. The Lean Mastery Suite of courses are interactive E-learning education courses designed to provide a Lean education to employees at all levels in the business enterprise and provide the guidelines for a successful Lean implementation.

Keith began his career in Public Accounting with Haskins and Sells, then a Big 8 accounting firm. After three years in public accounting Keith moved into private industry as an internal audit professional working for GTE, United Shoe Machinery, Data Terminal Systems, Wang Laboratories Inc, and Invensys. During his career Keith has performed financial and operational audits, fraud investigations, and acquisition audits at companies located throughout the world. Keith has lived and worked in Europe and also had responsibility for audit operations within the Pacific Rim for over ten years.

Keith made the transition from audit to operational management while at the Invensys Corporation where he studied Lean Enterprise concepts and became the Director of Lean Operations at the Invensys Metering Division and was responsible for the Lean transformations at over twenty manufacturing plants in North and South America, Europe, and Asia.

About Lean Enterprise Inc.

Lean Enterprise Inc. is a leading-edge consulting company that provides creative products and services for organizations in all industries (manufacturing, healthcare, service etc.) that are transitioning to Lean business processes. Initially formed with a mission to create a low-cost mechanism to educate everyone in the organization, Lean Enterprise Inc. today provides consulting and education services to numerous companies (including Fortune 500) , and has developed innovative distance learning products that are offered at 250+ universities and major corporations.

From the renowned Lean Mastery course that requires student ROI, the "Lean Mastery", "Lean Coach", Lean for the Office" and "Lean for Healthcare" WBT training modules were created to provide the low-cost, high-quality education needed for Lean concepts to flourish throughout the business world. Lean Enterprise Inc. has also created the innovative Establishing Offshore Operations course for those organizations planning to set up operations overseas. This course contains a comprehensive spreadsheet with hundreds of cost categories that need to be considered when planning an offshore move.

Known for their no-nonsense approach, Principals Keith Gilpatrick and Brian Furlong (authors of "The Elusive Lean Enterprise") are the company owners and they provide education or consulting services to the University of Akron, the Corporate College Lean Institute, University of Cincinnati, Youngstown State University, Kent State University, Maharishi University and many corporations. Their products or services have been provided to companies such as Bosch, FASCO Motors, Energizer, Goodyear Chemical, Goodrich, Snap-on Tools, Mercy Healthcare, Parker-Hannifin, KENCO, Curtiss Wright, Moen Corporation, Ingersoll Rand, Visiting Nurses Association, Beckett among many others.

Lean Enterprise Inc also develops on-line courses for third parties and provides low cost on-line hosting for courses through its Learning Management System.

You can learn more about Lean Enterprise Inc. and their unique products and services by visiting their website at www.leanvalue.com.

If you liked this book, you may be also interested in...

Corporate Intelligence Awareness: Securing the Competitive Edge

In this compelling new book by a former diplomat, you will learn the secrets (step by step) to developing an intelligence strategy by effective information gathering and analyzing, and then to delivering credible intelligence to senior management. Along the way, you will learn how to better read people and organizations and get them to open up and share information with you—all the while behaving in an ethical, legal manner. Understanding how intelligence is gathered and processed will keep you ahead of the game, protect your secrets, and secure your competitive edge!

ISBN: 1-895186-42-0 (hardcover)
ISBN: 1-895186-43-9 (PDF ebook)

Also available in other ebook formats. Order from your local bookseller, Amazon.com, or directly from the publisher at **http://www.mmpubs.com/cia**

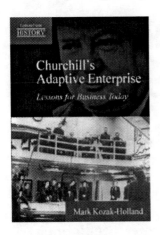

Churchill's Adaptive Enterprise: Lessons for Business Today

This book analyzes a period of time from World War II when Winston Churchill, one of history's most famous leaders, faced near defeat for the British in the face of sustained German attacks. The book describes the strategies he used to overcome incredible odds and turn the tide on the impending invasion. The historical analysis is done through a modern business and information technology lens, describing Churchill's actions and strategy using modern business tools and techniques. Aimed at business executives, IT managers, and project managers, the book extracts learnings from Churchill's experiences that can be applied to business problems today. Particular themes in the book are knowledge management, information portals, adaptive enterprises, and organizational agility.

Eric Hoffer Book Award (2007) Winner

ISBN: 1-895186-19-6   (paperback)
ISBN: 1-895186-20-X   (PDF ebook)

http://www.mmpubs.com/churchill

MEETING with SUCCESS

Tips and Techniques for Great Meetings

A New Book by Ida Shessel

Are People Finding Your Meetings Unproductive and Boring?

Turn ordinary discussions into focused, energetic sessions that produce positive results.

If you are a meeting leader or a participant who is looking for ways to get more out of every meeting you lead or attend, then this book is for you. It's filled with practical tips and techniques to help you improve your meetings.

You'll learn to spot the common problems and complaints that spell meeting disaster, how people who are game players can effect your meeting, fool-proof methods to motivate and inspire, and templates that show you how to achieve results. Learn to cope with annoying meeting situations, including problematic participants, and run focused, productive meetings.

ISBN: 1-897326-15-7   (paperback)
Also available in ebook formats.

http://www.mmpubs.com/

The Project Management Essentials Library

Managing
Smaller
Projects

"Simply put, this book is about helping people control smaller projects in a logical and effective way, and making the process run smoothly, and is indeed a success in achieving that goal."

IEE Engineering Management ;12/04)

Mike Watson

Award-winning trainer and PM Methodology guru

Managing Smaller Projects: A Practical Approach

So called "small projects" can have potentially alarming consequences if they go wrong, but their control is often left to chance. The solution is to adapt tried and tested project management techniques.

This book provides a low overhead, highly practical way of looking after small projects. It covers all the essential skills: from project start-up, to managing risk, quality and change, through to controlling the project with a simple control system. It cuts through the jargon of project management and provides a framework that is as useful to those lacking formal training, as it is to those who are skilled project managers and want to control smaller projects without the burden of bureaucracy.

Read this best-selling book from the U.K., now making its North American debut. *IEE Engineering Management* praises the book, noting that "Simply put, this book is about helping people control smaller projects in a logical and effective way, and making the process run smoothly, and is indeed a success in achieving that goal."

Available in print format. Order from your local bookseller, Amazon.com, or directly from the publisher at
www.mmpubs.com/msp

Edited by Kevin Aguanno, PMP, MAPM

The Project Management Essentials Library

Managing Agile Projects

Are you being asked to manage a project with unclear requirements, high levels of change, or a team using Extreme Programming or other Agile Methods?

If you are a project manager or team leader who is interested in learning the secrets of successfully controlling and delivering agile projects, then this is the book for you.

From learning how agile projects are different from traditional projects, to detailed guidance on a number of agile management techniques and how to introduce them onto your own projects, this book has the insider secrets from some of the industry experts – the visionaries who developed the agile methodologies in the first place.

ISBN: 1-895186-11-0   (paperback)
ISBN: 1-895186-12-9   (PDF ebook)

http://www.agilesecrets.com

Want to Get Ahead in Your Career?

Do you find yourself challenged by office politics, bad things happen-ing to good careers, dealing with the "big cheeses" at work, the need for effective networking skills, and keeping good working relation-ships with coworkers and bosses? *Winning the Rat Race at Work* is a unique book that provides you with case studies, interactive exercises, self-assessments, strategies, evaluations, and models for overcom-ing these workplace challenges. The book illustrates the stages of a career and the career choices that determine your future, empowering you to make positive changes.

Written by Peter R. Garber, the author of *100 Ways to Get on the Wrong Side of Your Boss*, this book is a must read for anyone interested in getting ahead in his or her career. You will want to keep a copy in your top desk drawer for ready reference whenever you find yourself in a challenging predica-ment at work.

ISBN: 1-895186-68-4   (paperback)
Also available in ebook formats. Order from your local bookseller, Amazon.com, or directly from the publisher at
http://www.mmpubs.com/rats

Need More Help with the Politics at Work?

100 Ways To Get On The Wrong Side Of Your Boss (And Strategies to Prevent You from Getting There!) was written for anyone who has ever been frustrated by his or her working relationship with the boss—and who hasn't ever felt this way! Bosses play a critically important role in your career success and getting on the wrong side of this important individual in your working life is not a good thing.

Each of these 100 Ways is designed to illustrate a particular problem that you may encounter when dealing with your boss and then an effective strategy to prevent this problem from reoccurring. You will learn how to deal more effectively with your boss in this fun and practical book filled with invaluable advice that can be utilized every day at work.

Written by Peter R. Garber, the author of *Winning the Rat Race at Work*, this book is a must read for anyone interested in getting ahead. You will want to keep a copy in your top desk drawer for ready reference whenever you find yourself in a challenging predicament at work.

ISBN: 1-895186-98-6   (paperback)
Also available in ebook formats. Order from your local bookseller, Amazon.com, or directly from the publisher at
http://www.InTroubleAtWork.com

Networking *for* Results

THE POWER *OF* PERSONAL CONTACT

In partnership with Michael J. Hughes, *The* Networking Guru, Multi-Media Publications Inc. has released a new series of books, ebooks, and audio books designed for business and sales professionals who want to get the most out of their networking events and help their career development.

Networking refers to the concept that each of us has a group or "network" of friends, associates and contacts as part of our on-going human activity that we can use to achieve certain objectives.

The *Networking for Results* series of products shows us how to think about networking strategically, and gives us step-by-step techniques for helping ourselves and those around us achieve our goals. By following these practices, we can greatly improve our personal networking effectiveness.

Visit **www.Networking-for-Results.com** for information on specific products in this series, to read free articles on networking skills, or to sign up for a free networking tips newsletter. Products are available from most book, ebook, and audiobook retailers, or directly from the publisher at **www.mmpubs.com**.

 **The Project Management Audio Library**

In a recent CEO survey, the leaders of today's largest corporations identified project management as the top skillset for tomorrow's leaders. In fact, many organizations place their top performers in project management roles to groom them for senior management positions. Project managers represent some of the busiest people around. They are the ones responsible for planning, executing, and controlling most major new business activities.

Expanding upon the successful *Project Management Essentials Library* series of print and electronic books, Multi-Media Publications has launched a new imprint called the *Project Management Audio Library*. Under this new imprint, MMP is publishing audiobooks and recorded seminars focused on professionals who manage individual projects, portfolios of projects, and strategic programmes. The series covers topics including agile project management, risk management, project closeout, interpersonal skills, and other related project management knowledge areas.

This is not going to be just the "same old stuff" on the critical path method, earned value, and resource levelling; rather, the series will have the latest tips and techniques from those who are at the cutting edge of project management research and real-world application.

www.PM-Audiobooks.com

Printed in the United States
91992LV00002B/58/A